Walking With God

A Collection of Poems

Elder Ralph E. Harris

Sovereign Grace Publications
Cullman, Alabama

WALKING WITH GOD: A COLLECTION OF POEMS
Published by Sovereign Grace Publications LLC
Post Office Box 1061
Cullman, Alabama 35056
www.sovgrace.net
sovgracepublications@gmail.com

The publisher gratefully acknowledges permission to reprint texts granted by the publishers and organizations footnoted on the following pages: 23, 39, 58, 59, 60, 91, 93, 151, 152, 153, 261, 276, 277, 278, and 306. Every effort has been made to secure current copyright permission information on the poems used. If any right has been infringed, the publisher pledges to make the correction in subsequent printings as the additional information is received.

ISBN 978-1-929635-23-8

Printed in the United States of America.

CONTENTS

FOREWORD

On the few occasions someone has approached me with the suggestion that I try my hand at composing hymns, I've quipped that I write poor poetry and even poorer music. The solicitor generally laughs, as do I, and it sounds like a well-refined attempt to feign humility...but it's not. The assessment is uncomfortably accurate.

In fact, I suspect that judgment is accurate in most cases. Aspiring poets may be common, but accomplished poets are rare. Those gifted souls who paint verbal portraits of sublime themes in memorable verse, captivating thought and energizing affection, are extraordinary blessings to the church of God. Elder Ralph Harris is such a poet.

Ralph Harris is one of the most prolific writers among contemporary Primitive Baptist ministers. It was my privilege two years ago to publish a significant portion of his prose in a devotional volume entitled *Day by Day*. I'm thankful now for the opportunity to add to that title this collection of poems for the devotional benefit of the individual and the potential benefit of the churches in terms of public worship.

Each generation of the church needs its poets and hymn writers. Since the 17th century hymn writing pioneer Isaac Watts, often called "the Father of English hymnody," a number of exceptionally talented poets have made valuable contributions to the sung worship of the church.

How impoverished would contemporary worship be without Watts' Christological gem "When I Survey the Wondrous Cross," or the theologically-rich "O God, Our Help in Ages Past"? After years of exposure to the substantive theology of Doddridge's "Grace 'Tis a Charming Sound" and Cowper's "God Moves in Mysterious Ways," Newton's Christ-centered "How Sweet the Name of Jesus Sounds," the experientially-resonant work of Fanny Crosby's "Blessed Assurance, Jesus is Mine," and the faith-building classic of Joseph Scriven "What A Friend We Have in Jesus," I could never be content with superficial, sentimental praise choruses. "How Firm a Foundation," "There is a Fountain," and "Nearer My God to Thee" do something for my soul that the frivolous repetition of "yes, Jesus, yes, yes, Jesus," with hands caressing the air, just doesn't do.

In his excellent volume *The Poetic Wonder of Isaac Watts*, Douglas Bond observes that contemporary Christian people desperately need to recover the kind of substantive theological poetry of the man who penned "Alas and Did My Savior Bleed" and "When I Can Read My Title Clear." He writes:

> Our world clambers after the latest thing, and…great poets such as Watts often get put in a box on the curb for the thrift store pickup…Our postmodern, post-Christian, post-biblical culture has almost totally dismissed what was called poetry in Watts' day. Few deny it: ours is a post-poetry culture. [1]

Why has the discipline of poetry declined in pop-culture? No doubt, the proliferation of technological gadgets with their innate form of fragmented communication via abbreviations and emoticons is a principal cause. The best-seller *The Shallows: What the Internet is Doing to Our Brains* is just one of several popular studies on the societal effects of our increasingly electronic world on the ability to think.[2] Of course, any creeping intellectual vacuum necessarily spawns a spiritual vacuum, for the soul is intrinsically tied to the understanding.

Bond, however, traces the declension in modern poetry to its literary source. He argues that the decline may be traced to Walt Whitman, "a man with new ideas that demanded a new form."[3] Like abstract art, Whitman's new poetry, called *vers libre*, rejects the classic literary goal of reflecting the beauty of objective truth and becomes a vehicle of subjective, self-expression. Conventional

---

[1] Douglas Bond, *The Poetic Wonder of Isaac Watts*, p. xix.
[2] By Nicholas Carr, published in 2010 by W. W. Norton & Co., Ltd.
[3] Bond, p. xx.

poetic structures like meter and rhyme, the qualities that make lyrics singable (and memorable), have no place in "free verse" poetry. This kind of poetry is called "flarf." Bond writes:

> One tragic result of Whitman and his imitators is that we have forfeited the ability to measure the quality of poetry, so free verse proliferates without censure as everyone and his cocker spaniel gets in touch with the poet within, including well-intentioned youthful worship leaders. There is little place for Watts in such a literary world. Ours is without a rudder, where poetry has no boundaries, no canvas, no walls, no arches, no vaulted ceilings—and, hence, no enduring grandeur. Today one can create verse and call it poetry by doing a Google search, then blending the results into lines of absurdity. And, yes, it has a name: *flarf*. Flarf poetry and its derivatives have redefined what poetry is.[4]

In such an increasingly intellectual- and soul-impoverished age, believers in the Lord Jesus Christ not only need to rediscover the substantive hymn-poems of antiquity, but also to discover the fresh contributions of contemporary Christians who follow in that same tradition. It is for that reason that I am glad to make this rich collection of soundly theological and richly experiential poems available to the Lord's people.

But there is a need even more basic and fundamental. Modern folk, especially Christian people, need to rediscover the importance of poetry, itself. I know of nothing so conducive to the fruitful Christian discipline of meditation as good poetry. More than once in my life, I've reached for a book of hymn-poems to breathe life into my languid faith and cold heart. The devotional benefit spawned by reflection on sublimely worded, theologically-sound lyrics cannot be overstated.

It was King George II that infamously exclaimed, "I hate all poets." The very discipline of writing verse seemed, to him, a waste of time. Many Muslims would agree. Poetry is disparaged in the *Qur'an* and discouraged in Islamic life and culture. In fact, Muhammad himself made some pretty harsh statements against

---

[4] Ibid. p. xxii.

poets and allegedly had some poets that had lampooned him in their poetry killed.

But Christianity has historically encouraged and prized its poets, especially the hymn-poets who write for the spiritual benefit of the average believer instead of the professional literary critic. With the emergence of Isaac Watts' hymn poems, the sung worship of Christians was revolutionized. Those godly men and women who have followed in his steps have left a living legacy of hymn poems that still benefit us today.

May we never take the poetic contributions of godly and doctrinally-sound Christians, like Ralph Harris, for granted. I do hope that publishers of hymnals will incorporate some of the best of these poems into future editions for use in the worship of the church. I hope preachers will, from time to time, incorporate some of these poems into their sermons. But most of all, I hope that ordinary believers, like us, will use this collection as a resource for the devotional discipline of daily meditation.

I have already spent several precious moments in communion with the Lord as I've readied these pages for print. I may not be equally adept as Elder Harris at writing poetry, but I can certainly read and use it as a springboard for fruitful meditation. I look forward to many more opportunities to reflect on the truth of God's word as I consult this collection again and again in the future.

Michael L. Gowens
September 2014
Cullman, Alabama

AUTHOR'S PREFACE

In December of 1986 I had an impression to see if I could compose a poem for the front cover of each issue of the *Advocate and Messenger* for the upcoming year. I of course had no way of knowing how this would turn out. I thought perhaps I would fail in the effort, but that there could be no harm in trying.

My first poem for that year was titled, "Walking With God." Hence, sometime later, when I had written enough poetry for a small volume, I decided to use that same title. The first compilation of the early collection of poems was largely the result of urging from Sister Loretta Lilly of Akron, Ohio. Without her encouragement I might never have done it.

As I began writing I had soon accumulated enough poems for 1987. But it obviously did not stop there. More poetry has continued to come to me from time to time ever since then, and a number of them developed into compositions too lengthy for the A&M cover, so I sent some of them to other Primitive Baptists publications. My attempts at poetry have continued for many years, and in my wildest dreams I could never have anticipated a volume of its present size.

Much of this poetry has come to me in the night, and many times I have arisen from a state of extreme drowsiness to write down a line, or perhaps a few lines, that I knew I probably would not remember if I waited until daylight to put them on paper. I have also many times jotted down a line or two in the night and the rest of the composition would come to me before I could get back to sleep, or perhaps the next day, or sometimes even days later.

Perhaps there is a lesson for us in this. If we use what the Lord gives us He will give us more. But if we bury our gifts they will never be useful to us or anyone else. More importantly, they will never bring glory to the Giver, and will eventually be taken away.

May all of us be blest to daily **walk with God.**

—Elder Ralph E. Harris

Walking With God

The Lord be praised! thus far we've come
On life's uneven road;
His grace has softened all our trials,
And helped us bear the load.

O may He lead us safely on,
As in His steps we plod,
So that our epitaph might read:
"He (She) humbly walked with God."

PART 1
THE CHARACTER OF GOD

God Still Reigns
When trouble comes 'tis good to know
The Lord still reigns on high;
And though perhaps He seems clean gone
He nonetheless is nigh.

He will not leave His trusting flock
To face the foe alone;
He'll keep them safely by His grace
And lead them gently on.

God's All-Seeing Eye
Oh troubled soul do not despair,
The eye of God sees all.
He knows our need before we ask,
And answers e're we call.

Though now the way seems e'er so dark,
To Him it all is plain;
In time we'll have a clearer view
And count our loss as gain.

A Faithful God

Worldly wealth is fleeting,
Temp'ral prospects dim,
But the Lord endureth—
May we trust in Him.

He will ne'er forsake us,
Nor betray our trust;
He is ever righteous,
Faithful, true and just.

He Knows Best

Oft'times we do not understand
The path that we must trod;
Yet we desire the providence
Which leads us nearer God.

We know not what the future holds
But in this truth we rest,
His way is always right and good,
For He knows what is best.

Our Refuge
The schemes of mortal man
Are built on sinking sand,
And soon they shall expire
When tested by the fire.

We must not put our trust
In objects made of dust.
Lord, let this be our plea,-
Our refuge is in Thee.

~~~

Peace Be Still
Almighty God of all the earth
And Ruler of the skies,
Thy pow'r alone canst still the wind
And calm our anxious sighs.

How soothing are Thy gracious words!
How sweet Thy "Peace be still"!
When all within bows humbly to
Thy holy, sov'reign will.[1]

~~~

[1] Composed during a storm.

God's Providence
God's providence toward us has been
A wonder to behold.
His gentle hand has guided us
Through storm, through heat and cold.

'Tis by His grace we stand or fall,
We're kept by pow'r Divine;
Thus at His throne we humbly bow,
And say, "The glory's Thine."

God Never Fails
We know not what the future holds
Except what God unveils,
But in this truth we all may rest,
His purpose never fails.

No matter what may come to pass,
God still is on His throne;
He cannot lie, He cannot fail,
Nor e're forsake His own.

All Glory to God
Our great God of love and mercy
Is a God of wonders too:
He can change a poor, vile sinner,
Melt his heart and make him new.

Vain are man's most grand achievements
When compared with power Divine:
Let all saints join in the anthem,
"All the glory, Lord, is Thine."

Idol Gods
Oh Thou self-exalting soul,
Tow'ring upward stout and bold,
God can see thy thin disguise,
And thy crumbling house of lies.

Thou whose gods are gain and self
Shall at last be all bereft.
Where will be thine idol gods
When thou sleepest 'neath the clods?

Reverent Majesty
Thy majesty, O gracious Lord
Exceeds our highest thought;
We stand amazed as we survey
The wonders Thou hast wrought.

O may we ever honor Thee
And Thy most holy law;
And may we ne'er invoke Thy name
Except in rev'rent awe!

A Powerful God

The minds of men abound with gods
Who try but always fail;
But heaven's God performs His will,
His might and pow'r prevail.

He showed His pow'r on Carmel's brow
When fire from heaven fell:
He foiled the cunning craftiness
Of wicked Jezebel.

The God who made the earth and sea
Can suffer no defeat;
He saves the heirs of grace divine
And makes the work complete.

Our Wonderful Creator

Our great Creator spoke the word,
And worlds began to be,
And all things had their being from
The breath of Deity.

He is a wise, omniscient God
Who numbers every hair;
He sees the tear upon our face
And knows what put it there.

He fills the vast expanse of space
With omnipresent might,
And rules o'er all created things
With justice, truth, and right.

The Lord Provides
Our gracious God abides,
And faithfully provides:
He knows our plight
both day and night
And constantly provides.

We can in Him confide,
And trust Him to provide:
He knows our need
before we plead
And graciously provides.

His Daily Providence
His Daily Providence
God sees the sparrow when it falls,
Though tiny in our sight;
He sees the earthworm when it crawls,
Though hidden from the light.

And we, to Him, are worth far more
Than these low creatures are:
The care He displays o'er and o'er
T'ward us is greater far.

His daily providence is sure,
His blessings never cease:
In this great truth may we endure
And walk with Him in peace.

Our Ever-present God

Our God is the God
Of the sunbeam's light,
As well as the God
Of the darkest night.

He's as much our God
When the clouds are low,
As He is when stars
In their splendor glow.

He's our God in joy
And when grief is sore,
And will always be
Till our journey's o'er.

～

Compared To God

No radiant sun is half so bright
As He who is the source of light.
A shooting star would be but dim
If e'er it were compared to Him.

The wisdom of this world is blind
Compared to God's eternal mind;
Its knowledge like a new-born youth
Compared to God's eternal truth.

The riches of all earth combined,
With all the gold that could be mined,
Is nothing to the quickened eye
Compared to wealth laid up on high.

～

God's Glory Acknowledged

The heavens show God's handiwork,
The earth bespeaks His skill:
His glory beams from ev'ry star,
From ev'ry rock and rill.

The quickened eye can see God's hand
In all created things;
In all His works of providence,
And in the grace it brings.

O, may we then acknowledge Him
In ev'ry thought and deed,
With childlike faith beseeching Him
To grant our ev'ry need.

~∞~

God Is Great

Our God is great, and He is good—
Just as the little children pray:
He keeps His humble servants safe
And guides them in the narrow way.

They are a special, chosen race
And they are precious in His sight;
His providence gives daily bread
And watches them both day and night.

They are secure in Christ their Lord
In Whom they are preserved and called
They serve Him with an unfeigned faith
And in His love they're oft' enthralled.

~∞~

Without Thee

Without Thee, Lord, the stars would fall,
Chaos would reign in earth and sky;
The glowworm could not give its light,
All nature would grow cold and die.

The dove would cease her plaintive call,
The fields and flow'rs would cease to bloom;
The light would swiftly flee away
Replaced by shades of endless gloom.

A blessing 'tis to us that Thou
Dost not forsake such worms as we,
We ' re so dependent on Thy pow'r
Without Thee, Lord, where would we be?

Only One True God

Thy Glory, Lord, exceeds by far
The luster of the brightest star.
Thy pow'r exceeds all else beside
And in that pow'r we may confide.

Thy wisdom shines from age to age
More brightly than the wisest sage.
Thy love toward men of unclean lips
No other love shall e'er eclipse.

Let heathen gods be multiplied
And in such whims let men confide,
To us there is but one true God;
'Twas He who made both sea and sod.

The Father's Great Hands
A child took father's hands in his
And said, "How big they are!"
Then father said, "Ah, yes, my child,
But God's are bigger far."

"How big, dear father, must they be?"
The child said with a groan.
"They're big enough, my precious child,
To hold each of His own."

"Upon the palms of His great hands
Is ev'ry heir engraved,
And since they cannot be erased,
They'll all, at last, be saved."

❧

Kept By His Power
God's pow'r took dust, the lowly dust,
And made it flesh and bone,
And that same pow'r didst raise the dead
And broke the heart of stone.

The God who spake and worlds appeared,
Who spake and calmed the sea,
With equal ease can also bring
Vile sinners to their knee.

'Tis this great God in whom we trust,
On Him we can depend;
The pow'r that kept us until now
Will keep us to the end.

❧

The Lord Still Reigns
Though earthly kings are soon removed
And others take their seat
The Lord still reigns and earth remains
The stool beneath His feet.

The Lord still reigns in majesty
In earth and sky and sea,
He reigns within the hearts of men,
He reigns eternally.

The Lord still reigns and we rejoice
That He is in control,
He'll always keep His little sheep
And bring them to the fold.

❦

God Is Faithful
God is faithful though we falter,
He is steadfast though we fall,
He is watchful though we slumber,
He is ruling over all.

He is faithful to His promise
Though we often break our vow,
He still loves us though we grieve Him
And we often wonder how.

He still lives though we are dying
He forever is the same
And in spite of all our failings
We'll forever praise His name.

❦

God's Faithfulness
God is faithful, truly faithful
Let us trust Him and obey...
He'll not leave us nor forsake us
Nor our confidence betray.

He is faithful when we fail Him
He is faithful when we fall
And through His unfailing kindness
He will save His people all.

Through His faithfulness and mercy
All our foes shall be put down
Thus where sin has sore abounded
Much more shall His grace abound.

❧

Let Us Reverence Him
Our foes are great, there is no doubt
But God is greater still...
He exercises full control
And does His sovereign will.

No man can stay His mighty hand
Or say, "What doest Thou?"
Before Him all the powers of hell
With fear and dread must bow.

Let us with reverence honor Him
And walk with Him in love
Immersed with heart and mind and soul
In gracious things above.

❧

None Else But God

I've seen the power of God displayed
In hearts and lives touched by His hand:
I've seen the blind receive their sight
And rebels changed at His command.

How else could wonders such as these
Be wrought among the sons of men?
Who else can do such wondrous deeds
And give new life where death had been?

Such wonders all around we see
And blest are we if we have known
That God alone deserves the praise
And still sits firm upon His throne.

God is Master

God is Master of the morning,
He is Master of the night.
Hence He rules in all creation
With an awful pow'r and might.

He is Master of the pauper,
He is Master of the king,
At His word the graves fly open
And cold death yields up its sting.

He is Master o'er the heavens
And o'er all its spacious parts;
Yet He stoops to love His people
And to dwell within their hearts.

Our Great Creator

God did form the towering mountains
And He made the desert plains;
Also made the flowing fountains
And the mighty bounding mains.

What a marvelous Creation!
And a Great Creator too!
He is due our adoration
And the best that we can do.

He hath made us for His glory
All His precepts to embrace,
And we love to hear the story
How He saved us by His grace.

❧

O, What a God is He!

Almighty in His works and ways;
Eternal, pure, and without days:
Let all the earth His goodness praise,
O, what a God is He!

He works and none can stay His hand,
He rules and reigns in every land
And princes bow at His command,
O, what a God is He!

Forever He doth rule and reign
And evil vies with Him in vain,
There is in Him no hint of stain,
O, what a God is He!

❧

A Mighty Refuge

A refuge is the Lord our God
And underneath are His great arms:
He keeps us as through life we plod
And helps us shun the devil's charms.

He is a Shield from ev'ry foe;
A Covert from the raging storm,
A Shelter from the ice and snow,
A Loving Sun to keep us warm.

If we are kept by His great hand
No power or force can do us harm;
But we through grace will bravely stand
While leaning on His mighty arm.

God's Creation

"The world is the Lord's
And the fulness thereof."
Upon it is stamped
The marks of His love.

Great beauty is seen
In its mountains and glades;
In its dazzling bouquets—
In it hues and its shades.

"All these were made
For His honor," says He,
And we should give honor
Where honor should be.

I Marvel
I marvel at the love of God
Exceeding human thought:
I gaze with wonder on the works
His mighty hands have wrought!

His wisdom makes me stand in awe,
His pow'r o'erwhelms my mind;
I tremble when I view His law
As wondrously Divine!

I marvel that a wretch like me
Should be a chosen heir,
And finally that I should see
That home above so fair!

More Trust and Submission Desired
O Thou whose voice the winds obey,
Whose might awakes the dead;
Whose pow'r turned water into wine,
And multiplied the bread.

Thy wond'rous pow'r is no less now
Than in the former years;
Thou still canst keep us safe from harm
And dry our troubled tears.

O may we learn to trust Thee more,
Thy precepts to fulfil,
And always be submissive to
Thy good and perfect will.

Adore Him All Ye Sons of Men

God works by purpose and design;
He knows the future in advance:
In His great plan there is no place
For happen-so or random chance.

He does His will in heav'n and earth
And none can stay His mighty hand:
He sees the sparrow when it falls
And nations bow at His command.

Though oft men war against His word
And in confusion rage and roar,
This only proves their wretchedness
And makes His glory shine the more.

He governs the affairs of men
And nothing takes Him by surprise:
No deed escapes His sov'reign gaze
Nor hides from His all-seeing eyes.

He beckons angels and they fly
Performing all He bids them do;
The pow'rs of hell submit with fear
And own Him altogether true.

Adore Him all ye sons of men,
He well deserves thy rev'rent praise:
Let ev'ry tongue confess His name
And anthems to His honor raise.

His Wondrous Works[2]

What wondrous things our Lord has done!
How awesome is His power!
He made the world and all it holds;
The tree, the grass, the flower.

He made the lofty mountain peaks
And crested them with snow;
He laid the rolling hills around
With rippling brooks below.

He made the mighty rivers flow
And charted out their course;
He made the clouds, the rain, the wind,
And He controls their force.

He made the mother's special love,
By her alone possessed,
And gave that precious little babe
She cradles on her breast.

He makes the trembling, quickened soul
Who calls to Him in prayer,
He gives the light by which they see
His glory everywhere.

Oh! who can count His wondrous works?
By men it can't be done.
We might as well attempt to count
The orbs beyond the sun.

O let us daily praise His name
With great humility,
For making all that's beautiful
And blessing us to see.

---

[2] Previously published in *The Christian Pathway*, June 1991. Used by permission.

Man's Hand Too Small

Man cannot make a universe
Nor put a star in space;
He cannot make a sun or moon.
And put it in its place.

No man can make the sun stand still
Nor make it start again:
Such things the God of heav'n can do
But not poor, feeble man.

Man can't create a grain of sand,
Much less a world like ours:
He neither has the knowledge nor
The power it requires.

No man can calm the raging seas
Nor still the mighty wind:
No man can stay the swelling tide
Nor cause the rain to end.

No man can raise the dead to life
Nor quicken any soul:
Man cannot make the blind to see
Nor make the sinner whole.

He cannot save the lost from hell
Nor make them loathe their sin
Can't make them see the dear old church
Nor long to enter in.

Such things require the work of God,
Man's hand is much too small.
May we commit our lives to Him
And crown Him Lord of all.

If There Were No God
If there were no God
There'd be no land nor sea;
There'd be no sun nor moon
And no eternity.

If there were no God
There'd be no Darling Son;
There'd be no praising Him,
No Christian race to run.

If there were no God
There'd be no one true church;
No precious truth to heed,
No inspired Word to search.

If there were no God
There'd be no baby's smile;
There'd be no "I love you's"
From husband, wife or child.

If there were no God
There'd be no peace and love;
There'd be no friendships dear,
There'd be no heav'n above.

If there were no God
There'd be no song to sing;
There'd be no you and me,
There'd be no anything.

God is in Control

God's wrath is seen throughout the earth
In many varied ways.
In fire and flood and earthquake too
This message He conveys.

The sins of men against their God
Like mighty mountains rise
And where shall they find shelter from
His great, all-seeing eyes?

In pestilence and dread disease
God makes His presence known,
But still we see defiance reign
In men with hearts of stone.

These mortal scenes shall still unfold
As long as earth remains
But what a comfort 'tis to know
That God still rules and reigns!

He knows each heir of grace divine
And holds them in His hand
And though they suffer here in time
Their final end is grand.

The plans of evil, godless men,
Whate'er those plans may be,
Cannot frustrate the works of God
Nor alter His decree.

He orders the affairs of men
And so maintains control,
That we may trust Him with our life
As well as with our soul.

Creation's Voice

The golden sunshine's radiant glow
Reminds us of the God of light;
The lightning and the thunder's peal
Remind us of His pow'r and might.

The gentle rain and morning dew
Both show His loving providence;
Each hour we live bespeaks that He
Has been to us a sure defense.

The rushing river's constant flow
Declares God's never-failing grace,
Reminding us how frail we are
And how we need to seek His face.

The fertile fields, the fruitful vine,
Show forth the bounties of His hand
And bring to mind the riches of
A better and more joyful land.

The rising sun, the budding flow'r,
Declare a resurrection morn,
When saints are carried to the skies
And glory doth their heads adorn.

The painted sunset brings to mind
That life on earth is but a span;
The evening shades speak loud and clear
That we should labor while we can.

O lift thine eyes and look around
And hear creation's clarion voice,
Instructing us in things Divine
And saying, "In the Lord rejoice!"

The Lord Knows Why

God lets the streams and lakes dry up
And all the fish to die;
Such things He oft' doth not prevent
And lets us wonder why.

We see a little one abused,
We hear their plaintive cry;
Their little heart is left to bleed—
We're left to wonder why.

The best folks often suffer most.
On beds of pain they lie,
And as they linger on for years
We sadly wonder why.

We see the wicked prospering
And see them riding high;
While some, like Laz'rus, beg for bread,
And we say, "Why, Lord, why?"

The saints cannot live free of sin
No matter how they try;
And as the battle rages on
They sometimes wonder why.

Injustice comes and godly souls
Desire from earth to fly,
But they are left to struggle on
And often wonder why.

'Tis good to know there is a God
Who hears our ev'ry sigh;
And though we oft' don't understand,
HE knows the reason why.

The Unfathomable God

How vast is this great universe—
Too vast to comprehend!
No glass can view its farthest point
Nor find where it begins.

And thus it is with all God's works;
Men cannot fathom them;
They cannot grasp His pow'r and might
And none can measure Him.

Men have no right to question God
And say, "What doest Thou?"—
To dictate what He "ought" to do,
Nor when, nor where, nor how.

Men ought to always keep in mind
That they are worms of dust,
And what He does—whate'er it be—
Is always pure and just.

They do not have a single pow'r
That did not come from Him;
And He can in a moment's time
Remove it all from them.

He holds their life within His hand
And gives them ev'ry breath,
And His sustaining hand withdrawn
Would bring them instant death.

How foolish do vile men appear
When in their haughty pride,
They vaunt themselves above the Lord
And seek to be His guide.

Before His feet each knee must bow
When in the final day
He wafts His people to the skies
And sends the goats away.

How humble ought we all to be
Before this mighty King
For since He's been so good to us
We owe Him everything.

<hr/>

God—A Timeless Being

Thru timeless ages God foreknew
Each heir of grace divine,
And bound them in His cov'nant love
By wise and sure design.

He knew in ev'ry fine detail
The life of ev'ry man;
And knew before He made the world
Each place their feet would stand.

For all eternity He knew—
Forever He has known—
All things that ever would transpire,
Each seed that would be sown.

God is a timeless Entity,
Eternally the same;
Incomprehensible is He
And rev'rend is His name.

How great and wise a God is this!
O let us bow in awe!
And humbly follow Him in faith,
Abiding in His law.

He Knows All Things

Before the world was ever formed
The Lord knew ev'ry heir of grace;
He knew the color of their skin
And ev'ry feature of their face.

He knew each thought each one would think
And ev'ry word each one would speak,
Where each of them would dwell, and when,
Their ev'ry valley, ev'ry peak.

He knew each pain they e'er would feel,
Each heartache, grief or doubt;
He knew each conflict they would face
And how, at last, it would turn out.

Blind unbelief cannot embrace
So great and wise a God as this,
'Tis faith alone that looks to Him
And longs for heav'nly life and bliss.

How comforting by faith to know
We have a God so great and wise
Who knew all things and has all pow'r
And ne'er is taken by surprise.

He always occupies the throne
And rules by ancient, sure design;
He wields a calm and sure control
For all eternity and time.

Tis good to know that in the end
God's purpose will have been worked out,
And great will be the day when He
Descends from heaven with a shout.

God's Mercy Endures[3]

How feebly do we serve the Lord!
And all we do seems so impure;
Our only hope lies in this truth,
His mercy doth for e'er endure.

Our sins like mountains seem to rise
But God in Christ provides the cure;
Because of His undying love
His mercy doth for e'er endure.

We oft may drink a bitter cup
And feel quite low and insecure;
Yet in this truth we may confide,
God's mercy doth for e'er endure.

When friends grow cold and prove untrue
This truth remains forever sure,
The Lord will ne'er forsake His sheep,
His mercy doth for e'er endure.

All earthly things will soon decay
And happiness we can't ensure;
But in this promise we find peace,
God's mercy doth for e'er endure.

As we near death, as all must do,
And earthly joys are growing fewer,
Great comfort will be found in this,
God's mercy doth for e'er endure.

When all is done and earth is passed
And we in heaven are secured,
We then will rest in this great truth,
God's mercy hath for e'er endured.

---

[3] From Psalm 136:1-26

The Artistry of God

The artistry of God above
From all creation clearly shines
Through all the highest elements
And in the lowest, darkest climes.

The feathered bird with colors bright
Adorned with beauty great and rare
Owes all its glory to the God
Who spreads the rainbows thru the air.

Each sunset is a product of
That hand from whence all beauties flow,
It bathes the sky from pole to pole
With num'rous hues and shades of gold.

What beauty God hath with us blest
To give us pleasure midst our grief
For ne'er are troubles so severe
That beauty cannot bring relief.

But though the earth and sky and sea
God's handiwork so well displays,
The beauties of the world to come
Will far exceed these nether sprays.

There'll be no scenes of ugliness
To mar the beauty of that place
And O what beauty it will be
To view our Savior face to face.

God Alone These Works Performs

Who gives the flowers their grand design
And plants them all throughout the earth?
Who stays the bottles of the skies
And knows when all the hinds give birth?

Who forms the dew and sends the rain
And paints the sky each day anew?
Who makes the desert to appear
Where once the shrubs and flowers grew?

Who holds this vast domain called Earth
And all its dwellers in His hand?
Who hides His truth from carnal minds
Yet lifts the veil at His command?

Who sets the bounds of raging seas
And calms the waters with His breath?
Who cheers the souls of dying saints
And holds the keys of hell and death?

Who turns the hearts of kings and queens
And brings to naught the great and strong?
Who wipes away the mourner's tears
And gives instead a thankful song?

Who holds the wicked foe at bay
And will not let his schemes prevail?
Who has all power in His hands
And cannot falter, faint or fail?

Who makes a sinner bow his head
And cry for mercy from above?
Who takes the hatred from his heart
And in its place gives peace and love?

'Tis God alone these works perform.
How mighty are His works and ways!
And 'tis because these things are true
That He alone deserves our praise.

God's Greatness

Our God is great—supremely great,
Too great for human tongue to tell:
So great He made the numerous worlds...
And all He did—He did it well.

His greatness shines throughout the earth
In everything His hand has made:
He did it all by His great power
Without the slightest help or aid.

So great is He that He can speak
And bring to pass whate'er He please,
Ev'n if it be to make the light
Or to divide the earth and seas.

So great is He that He can raise
The long dead from the sleeping tomb
Or make a long dry seed to grow
And flowers of spring to gaily bloom.

How great our loving God must be
To quicken those who're dead in sin...
To make them hate what they once loved
And praise Him for His grace within!

Yes, God is great, and He is good,
Just as the little children pray;
For He supplies us daily bread
And keeps us all along the way.

His greatness all His saints may trust
To keep them till their lives are o'er;
And then to take them home with Him
To praise His greatness ever more.

Our Sovereign God
O gracious Lord omnipotent
No pow'r can stay Thy hand;
Before Thee kings must cast their crowns
And bow at Thy command.

Thy rule is over ail the earth,
In heav'n and all of space;
Thy sovereignty is known and felt
By saints of ev'ry race.

There is no land, e'er so remote,
Where Thy great voice is mute;
And sage or seer has never lived
Who could Thy word refute.

Thou art from everlasting and
Forever Thou shall reign:
And magistrates, however great,
No pow'r o'er Thee shall gain.

Compared to Thee we feeble worms
Are as a wisp of smoke;
And Thy eternal, fixed decrees
Such worms cannot revoke.

Thou art just such a sovereign Lord
As poor vile sinners need,
For Thou alone canst reach our case
And for us intercede.

O let us praise Thee evermore
Almighty God supreme;
And may the wonders of Thy grace
Be our eternal theme.

~~~

O What a Mighty God is He
This stately orb on which we dwell
Did not itself create;
But it was made by power divine,
By wisdom good and great.

God did but speak and it appeared,
As did the starry skies;
And then He made all creeping things,
He made the bird that flies.

He made the rivers and the streams,
The oceans deep and wide;
He made the fish and mighty whales
Therein to e'er reside.

From dust he made an upright man
And then made him a mate;
And so by His great power alone
All things He did create.

O what a mighty God is He
Deserving all our praise;
By Him our very lives consist,
To Him belongs our days.

We could not draw another breath
If He did not sustain;
Our vapor-thin existence here
And full control maintain.

Let all His saints acknowledge Him
In all they say and do
And go relying on His grace
Until their days are through.

〰〰

Truth Old and New
Thy knowledge, Lord, the depths thereof!
We stand in awe of Thee!
Thy wisdom far exceeds our thought,
Its scope we dimly see.

Omniscience doth in Thee reside,
Omnipotence is Thine;
Thou art an omnipresent God
And ev'ry whit Divine.

One God, yet Oh! In persons three,
A myst'ry, yet 'tis true:
'Tis truth as old as God Himself
Yet always fresh and new.

〰〰

He Is Not Weak[4]

God is not weak, as some declare;
He rules and reigns on High.
He cannot be discouraged, and,
He cannot faint or die.

His sov'reign hand cannot be stayed,
Nor can His purpose fail;
He does His will in heav'n and earth,
In every hill and dale.

His majesty is glorified
In all created things;
And praise is rendered to His name
Each time a sparrow sings.

If tongues of men and angels ceased,
The stones would shout His praise;
If birds should hush their tuneful strains,
The stars would anthems raise!

There is no place in earth or heav'n
The voice of praise is mute;
It reaches to the farthest shore
And issues from the brute.

No Gadarene was e'er so wild,
Grace could not change his mind;
No Saul of Tarsus so enraged
God could not strike him blind.

He is the same from day to day,
His years can never fail;
He is not weak, as some contend,
His pow'r shall e're prevail.

---

[4] Previously published in *The Baptist Witness*, January 1991. Used by permission.

PART 2
SALVATION BY GRACE

This Precious Word
To save His people from their sins,
Christ Jesus came to earth;
So great a love no tongue can tell,
Nor estimate its worth.

God's servants nigh two thousand years
Have preached this precious word,
Yet they could not declare the whole —
The half has not been heard.

Undiminished Grace
Almighty God, abundant grace
Is treasured up in Thee,
And freely giv'n throughout the years
To sinners such as me.

But though bestowed on millions past,
There is no less supply;
Thy well of mercy still is full,
It never shall run dry.

An Unworkable Scheme
Within the carnal heart of man
There lurks a self-exalting plan
Which says that he can hide his sin
By simply letting Jesus in.

But if the word of God is true
Then such a scheme would never do,
For men a fatal path will trace
Unless delivered by free grace.

All Joy Traced To God
The Lord in mercy gave me sight,
And killed me to the love of sin;
He brought me to the source of light,
And gave me hope where fear had been.

Within my mouth a song He placed;
A song of praises to His name.
Thus all my joys to Him are traced,
Who took my sin and bore my shame.

Preserved By Grace
Great is our need, O gracious Lord,
And great is Thy supply:
Sad were our end, Lord, were it not
For Thine all-seeing eye.

T'was by Thy love Thou didst endure
The wrath that we deserved;
Tis by Thy pow'r that we are kept,
And by Thy grace preserved.

Hope in Christ Alone
O Lord, before Thy feet I fall,
In deep humility;
My sin I constantly recall,
Its stain is plain to see.

In this old flesh is nothing good?
This truth I sadly own;
And all my hope is in Thy blood
And righteousness alone.

No Condemnation
Men are poor obdurate dustworms,
Ruined entirely by the fall;
Void of all true Christian virtue,
Full of bitterness and gall.

But when Christ indwells His people
They become new creatures then,
Free from final condemnation,
Just as though they had no sin.

Death and Hell Conquered
"O grave, where is thy victory?
O death, where is thy sting?"
These words proclaim our Lord's success
As our triumphant King.

When He arose from Joseph's tomb
He conquered death and hell;
And all the saints at last shall rise,
With Him to ever dwell.

The Lord Shall Save His People
'Tis often said, "God *wants* to save,
If we'll but let Him in."
"If we'll submit to Him," some say,
"A good work He'll begin."

But Matthew one, and twenty one,
Cannot be swept aside;
The Lord shall save His people all,
Their debt He satisfied.

He works by purpose and by grace,
By promise firm, secure;
He knows His own elect, and this
Foundation standeth sure.

Monuments of Grace
God's dear elect are richly blest,—
All monuments of grace:
Snatched as an ember from the flames,
A holier path to trace.

Bought by the pure and spotless blood
From dear Emmanuel's veins,
The saint now dwells in stately court
And with his Savior reigns.

An Unbreakable Covenant
The Lord has promised His elect
He'll never leave them nor forsake
The covenant He made with them
He cannot alter, void nor break.

What He hath promised is as sure
As though it were already done;
And thus His people shall be saved
Without the loss of even one.

A Method Divine
How can a wretch so vile as me
Enjoy a blest eternity?
'Tis by a method all Divine,
And not by any works of mine.

If in the judgment all we brought
Were righteous deeds that we had wrought,
Our doom would surely then be sealed,
Our sentence could not be repealed.

But if we stand with Priestly dress
Clothed in our Lord's pure righteousness,
Our Father will pronounce us blest,
And give us an eternal rest.

How Great Thy Love!

How great Thy love, O gracious Lord,
Unto Thy dear, elected throng!
A love we cannot comprehend,
It is so large, so firm, so strong!

We never could deserve such love
In our corrupt and fallen state;
No works that we could e'er perform
Would merit love so true, so great.

Behold, the manner of His love!
That worms like we should be so blest
As to be saved by sov'reign grace
And be as "sons of God" addressed.

Who Can Condemn? — Romans 8:31-39

If God be on our side none can
Effectively oppose,
For He will give us grace to rise
Above our fiercest foes.

Who can condemn God's dear elect?
It is His Son that died!
Or who can bring a single charge?
'Tis God that justified.

Christ interceeds for them in heav'n
And they are quite secure.
No pow'r can separate their bond;
His love to them is sure.

I Owe My Savior Everything

I owe the Lord my everything
For what He's done for me;
He's made of me a priest and king,
A man of royalty.

When I was in a state of death
He quickened my vile heart;
He brought me to His house of love,
His bounties to impart.

Should I not then extol His name
Until my dying breath?
For He bore all my sin and shame
And saved me by His death.

✦

1 Cor. 2:14 — John 8:47

The natur'l man receiveth not
The things in which the saints delight.
He views them as mere foolishness
And turns from all things pure and right.

He cannot know these precious things.
To him they have not been revealed
And if the Spirit gives no light
They shall remain from him concealed.

Those quickened souls who are of God
Do hear His words and joy therein,
But those who have no part in Him
Despise His words and die in sin.

✦

Our Blessed Savior

Though we by nature are unclean
And have no righteousness,
We have a blessed Go-between
Who condescends to bless.

By His obedience and blood
We stand in Him complete,
In view of which we seek to live
At His beloved feet.

O may we never cease to praise
His worthy, matchless name;
May we His pure example trace
And emulate the same.

He Intervened

If God had never touched our heart
We had remained in sin;
The world would be our chief delight
And hell would be our end.

We'd miss the blessed privilege
Of Christian fellowship,
And all the joys of praising Christ
With heart, and life and lip.

The Lord be praised, He intervened
And opened our blind eyes,
He gave us title to His love
And mansions in the skies.

'Twas He

If not deceived I love the Lord,
But I can plainly see,
No credit can I claim for this—
'Twas He who first loved me.

'Twas He who wrote my name above
In His eternal Book;
'Twas He who paid redemption's price
When all my sins He took.

Predestination—praise His name—
Insured my final rest;
His precious promises declared
I'd be forever blest.

What Wondrous Grace!

Why would a God so pure and good
Show favor to such worms as we?
A myst'ry 'tis, that we should be
The objects of a love so free.

How strange that He should condescend
To write His laws within our heart;
And so imbed His Spirit there
That it can never from us part.

What wondrous grace! What boundless love!
Above our pow'rs to comprehend;
We'll never know the half of this
Until our souls to heav'n ascend.

From Nature to Grace
No mortal tongue can fully tell
The wretchedness of fallen man;
By nature he is bent t'ward hell
And cannot raise himself again.

Ere he can drink the heav'nly wine
His carnal will must be subdued,
The Lord must give him life divine,
His wicked heart must be renewed.

We love the Lord, 'tis very true,
Because, praise be, He loved us first;
His grace created us anew
And gave to us a heav'nly thirst.

Who Maketh Thee to Differ?
(1 Cor. 4:7)
Who maketh thee to differ from
All others o'er the land?
And what hast thou of any worth
That came not from God's hand?

Why should we glory, then, as though
Our gifts came not from Him?
We ought to give Him all the praise
For He gave all of them.

All glory to the Lamb be giv'n,
To Him it all belongs.
O may we crown Him Lord of all
And praise Him with our songs.

How Great a Thing

How great a thing is life Divine
No mortal tongue can tell!
It is a treasure none can buy—
A gift that none would sell.

How great a thing is God's pure love
Bestowed on sinners vile,
Through His eternal Holy Son
In whom there is no guile!

How great a thing 'twill be at last
To dwell in perfect peace,
Where Christ is ever our delight
And pleasures never cease!

Alone In Thee

O Lord, how vile a wretch am I!
And this my single plea;
The only righteousness I have
Resides alone in Thee.

Alone in Thee is all my hope,
Thou art my all in all,
And when I think how great Thou art
Upon my face I fall.

For all the future, O my Lord,
I trust in Thee alone
To see me through the vale of death
And then to waft me home.

By Virtue Of Grace

God, in His perfect love,
Embraced a chosen band,
And by grace secured their place
In heaven's happy land.

He sent His precious Son
To suffer, bleed and die,
To put away His people's sins
And justice satisfy.

By virtue of His grace
Vast numbers shall at last
Enjoy an endless day of peace
When earthly cares are past.

❦

Divine Election

In Christ the saints were chosen
From all eternity,
Not by their deeds or merits
But by Divine decree.

How grand, this great election!
Though frowned upon by men;
It designates the number
Who're saved from all their sin.

Without divine election
Not one in heav'n would be
Thank God for His affection
And for His grand decree!

❦

O, What a Foundation!

Not all the powers of evil
In earth and hell combined
Can overthrow God's purpose
Or make Him change His mind.

His counsels are eternal
And ever wise and sure;
They are more firm than granite
And ever shall endure.

His word cannot be broken;
His hand cannot be staid;
O, what a firm foundation
His mighty pow'r has laid!

∿∿

Christ My Only Righteousness

In Thy great mercy, Lord, I trust,
To works I cannot cling.
In me, that is, within my flesh,
There dwelleth no good thing.

Christ is my only righteousness,
None other can I plead;
No human merit can supply
A wretched sinner's need.

If I no Mediator had,
How sad my lot had been!
But Jesus paid my awful debt
And put away my sin.

∿∿

Secure in God's Hand
The Lord knows ev'ry heir of grace
And holds them in His hand;
He has prepared for them a place
In heaven's peaceful land.

Not one of them shall e'er be lost
Or from His flock be culled;
Their life is hid with Christ in God—
This cannot be annulled.

By cov'nant grace they are secured
And bound by changeless love;
And all at last shall be raised up
To happy realms above.

The Heirs of Grace
Long in the past, in God's eternal mind
His own elect He did in cov'nant bind;
Loved them with love no mortal can express
And keeps them all secure within His breast.

Each one He calls, in time from nature's night
Gives them new life, new hearing and new sight;
Will not desert them, nor will He forsake
But will receive them all for Jesus' sake.

Heav'n is assured to all these heirs of grace
Christ hath prepared in heav'n for them a place;
Soon all shall rise, and no, it won't be long,
T'will then be gathered 'round God's gracious throne.

Mighty to Save—Isaiah 63:1

"Mighty to save,"—God needs no help
Nor can poor man assist.
God saves His people by His grace
And they cannot resist.

He plants His Spirit deep within
And gives them a new heart:
A heart that loves Him and His saints
And will not from them part.

"Mighty to save" from all the foes
That greet them on their way,
And brings them safely through life's woes
To Heaven's blissful day.

Favors So Divine

Lord Almighty, condescending
To a sinner such as me,
Feebly I am comprehending
What a debt I owe to Thee.

Sinners, for their sins atoning?
Such a thing can never be!
Not our toils, nor deepest groaning:
Only Christ could set us free.

All our sins, He freely bore them,
Let our voices all combine
As we ever more adore Him
For His favors so divine.

If He Had Left Us

We never would have loved God's name
If He had not His work begun,
And ne'er would we have felt our shame
If He had ne'er revealed His Son.

We never would have sought His ways
If He had left us in our sin,
And ne'er would we have sung His praise
Had He not put new life within.

Heav'n never would have been our home
If Jesus ne'er had paid our debt,
But now there's hope beyond the tomb
And there our hearts are firmly set.

God's Rich Grace

It was by God's rich grace alone
That I was brought to see
My need of His redeeming love—
My sin and poverty.

My eyes did not behold Him till
He opened them to see,
And from that day His grace became
My one and only plea.

O may I ne'er lose sight of this—
E'er precious may it be,
Till that same grace has brought me home
His lovely face to see!

Sinless Only In Christ[1]
I'm born of man who failed to stand;
Who broke, in Eden, God's command,
And now all flesh is sinking sand
For we are full of sin.

I entertain no prospects vain
That to a state I'll ere' attain
While dwelling on these shores mundane
In which I have no sin.

But if my Lord upon the tree
Did bleed and die for wretched me,
Then one day I will sinless be
Through Him who bore my sin.

Imputed is His righteousness
To those dear souls He chose to bless,
And one sweet day they shall attest,
"Praise God! We have no sin."

---

[1] Previously published in *The Baptist Witness*, November 1990. Used by permission.

Romans 8:29-34[2]

Those whom the Lord foreknew in love,
He also did predestinate;
And these He calls by sov'reign grace,
In His own time, —He's never late.

And whom He calls from nature's night
He justifies and draws them nigh;
And those He freely justifies
He by and by will glorify.

What shall we say then to these things
Concerning those for whom Christ died?
Their sins were laid on Him, and now
God's justice has been satisfied.

A Royal Line[3]

Foreknown and loved, O Lord, are thine,
A priestly and a royal line;
Joint-heirs with Christ by heav'nly birth,
Their wealth exceeds the kings of earth.

In heav'n they have a place reserved
Which in themselves they ne'er deserved;
T'was by God's free and sov'reign grace
That Christ prepared for them a place.

He'll come again some glorious day
To waft this chosen band away
To realms of endless peace and joy
Where none can e'er again annoy.

---

[2] Previously published in *The Pathway of Truth*, December 1992. Used by permission.
[3] Ibid. February 1993.

God's Power[4]

God made the worlds by pow'r Divine
And all that in them is,
Without the aid of flesh and blood,
Thus all the glory's His.

He also makes repentant souls
Who plead at mercy's door;
And though He has no help from man
He does it o'er and o'er.

He does not ask us to assist
In giving heav'nly birth;
But He performs that gracious work
Just like He made the earth.

The pow'r that made the sun to shine
Enlightens ev'ry soul
Whose name is graciously inscribed
On heaven's sacred scroll.

The pow'r by which He raised our Lord
When three full days had passed,
Will raise up ev'ry heir of grace
And take them home at last.

---

4 Ibid. March 1993.

From Nature to Grace

By nature man is mean and vile,
Self-centered, proud and vain;
He loves to have the world's applause
And counts its wealth as gain.

But when the Holy Spirit hath
Performed a work of grace,
The sinner sees his wretchedness
And loathes his awful case.

The vanity of temp'ral things
He sees with quickened sight,
And falling down on trembling knees,
He begs for grace and light.

Then Christ reveals His righteousness,
And says, "I bore thy sins."
A sense of pardon is bestowed
And peace is wrought within.

The child of grace then leaps for joy
For what he understands,
And seeks to show his gratitude
By keeping God's commands.

~~~

An All-Sufficient Savior

Christ the all-sufficient Savior,
All His children's need supplies;
In His righteousness and bloodshed
All their hope of Heaven lies.

By His efficacious suff'rings
All the law's demands He met;
Took their sentence to Golgotha,
Bore their sins and paid their debt.

61

Equal to the wound they carried,
Gilead's Balm was well applied;
Thus the plaster Christ provided
Hid that which they could not hide.

With man's sin in Eden's garden
Came travailing pains in birth.
With the soul-travail of Jesus
Came salvation to the earth.

Did the curse come in with Adam,
By the snare the serpent laid?
So Christ died by crucifixion;
For His own, a curse was made.

Adam's sin brought in subjection,
Curses, fetters, hate and pain;
Thus was Jesus made of woman,
Under law, and man's disdain.

With the fall came in distresses
Such as thistles, briars and thorns;
Thus a crown of thorns was plaited
By which Christ's dear brow was torn.

Heat and sweat also befell us
When God's wrath came like a flood;
Thus did Jesus sweat in anguish
As it were great drops of blood.

Sorrow came with man's rebellion,
Grief and ruin, war and strife:
Thus acquainted was the Savior
With the sorrows of this life.

Did death come with Eve's transgression
When she yielded to the foe?
Thus obedient was the Savior
To this messenger of woe.

Thus His work is all-sufficient,
Plaster suited to the wound.
Blest be God for Christ the Savior,
May each heart in praise be tuned!

No One but God

When one is dead in sin and strife,
No one but God can give him life.
Though spires ascend to lofty perch,
No one but God can build a church.

When darkness thick beclouds our sight,
No one but God can give us light.
When truth we seek on bended knee,
No one but God can make us see.

When sorely these poor souls are tried,
No one but God can stem the tide.
When trouble rises like a wave,
No one but God has pow'r to save.

When sinking down in heavy mire,
No one but God can raise us high'r.
From life's demands and daily stress,
No one but God can give us rest.

Though we may toil our seed to sow,
No one but God can make them grow.
When everything is done and said,
No one but God can give us bread.

When to death's chilly stream we come,
No one but God can take us home;
And when we reach that bliss ere long,
No one but God will be our song.

His Precious Blood
If we could shed a million tears
In anguish for our sin,
It could not purge a single stain
Nor make us pure within.

'Twas Christ who died and bore our sins,
And Justice satisfied,
Who now in heaven intercedes
At His dear Father's side.

No agent short of Jesus' blood
Could pay the debt we owed,
Nor fit us for the realms of bliss,
The place of God's abode.

To His own blood and righteousness
We owe each joy Divine,
So may this be our daily song
The glory, Lord, is Thine.

What is Man?

O what is man, poor puny man,
That God should favor show?
By nature man is dead in sin
And is God's bitter foe.

O what is man that heaven's God
Should of him mindful be?
He is a product of the dust
And filled with vanity.

Consider, man, just what thou art
When left to self alone;
Thy carnal mind is enmity
Thy heart like flinty stone.

God is as high above thee, man
As heaven is the earth,
And without Him thou art undone,
Thy glory of no worth.

Why dost thou boast, O wretched man,
Thou fading flower of grass?
Where wilt thou be tomorrow, man?
Thy moments swiftly pass.

What wilt thou do, O feeble man,
When thou art faced with death?
Wilt thou praise God, or howl with fear,
When breathing thy last breath?

It profits not to vaunt thyself
And boast of all thy pow'r;
Thou canst not stop the march of tune
Nor shake the final hour.

Thou soon wilt face thy Maker, man,
And then what wilt thou do?
Thou canst not fool thy Maker, and,
He knows thee through and through

O may we mortals who fear God
Bow humbly at His throne,
Acknowledging our helplessness
And trusting Him alone.

We have no goodness of our own,
Christ is our righteousness,
And only for His sake doth God
Now condescend to bless.

Covenant Grace

God foreknew in cov'nant grace
His elect, a chosen race;
Sent His Son to save them all
From the curse of Adam's fall;
These He calls and justifies,
Makes them pure in heaven's eyes.

Since the world first saw the dawn
Many days have come and gone,
Drawing nearer to the day
When the saints shall fly away
To the land of perfect peace
Where their joys shall never cease.

Till that day they're kept secure
And by grace they shall endure;
All their needs shall be supplied
And in Christ they shall abide;

Many sorrows they must face
But He gives sufficient grace.

Here they serve a faithful God
And will sometimes feel His rod
For they need His chast'ning hand
When they err from His command;
Thus His love to them He shows
And their rev'rence for Him grows.

What a peace on earth is their's
For they know He truly cares
And will never do them wrong
But will with them suffer long;
And their life He'll richly bless
Till in heav'n their soul shall rest.

Great Blessings to God's People

How greatly blest are those who know
And love God's sovereign grace,
Who understands that He will save
His loved and chosen race!

They know that ere the world was made
His people were foreknown,
And in His great electing love
He claimed them as His own.

His great foundation standeth sure,
He knows them that are His
And to these meek and lowly lambs
How great a truth this is!

They feel their utter helplessness
Apart from saving grace;
And know that nothing short of this
Will reach their lowly case.

Their hope is in their Savior Christ,
They trust in Him alone,
For life and peace and righteousness,
They have none of their own.

They long to praise Him while they live
For all He's done for them;
They know from whence these treasures come
They owe it all to Him.

Their hope burns bright for heaven's world
Where joys shall never cease;
And saints arrayed in robes of white
Have never-ending peace.

Our Gracious Lord
What wondrous grace the Lord has shown
To mortals here below!
He dwelt amidst a fallen race
And suffered pain and woe.

He healed the sick and raised the dead
And cheered the frail and weak,
He preached the gospel to the poor
And made the dumb to speak.

He kept the law to ev'ry jot,
Its ev'ry line fulfilled;
And counts His righteousness as ours
Just as the Father willed.

He suffered death at wicked hands
And three days after rose;
He conquered death for all His saints,
Defeating all their foes.

He bore the wrath that we were due,
A debt no tongue can tell,
And when He paid the utmost price
His Father deemed it well.

No charge can any creature lay
To those for whom He died,
'Tis Christ who paid redemption's price,
'Tis He who justified.

He sits enthroned at God's right hand
And there He intercedes
For ev'ry soul who humbly bows
And to the Father pleads.

There is a day, a glorious day,
When saints to glory rise
To sweetly dwell with this great King
Forever in the skies.

Yes, There is Hope
Oh, is there hope for such a wretch,
For such a wretch as I?
Shall I see Jesus face to face
When I am called to die?

Yes, there is hope, a blessed hope,
For sinners such as we
In Jesus' blood and righteousness!
Oh, did He die for me?

If *sinners* were by Him redeemed
Then, yes, there's hope for me,
And I desire His soon return!
Oh, will He come for me?

I love my Savior's precious name
And long with Him to be,
And if I'm not His trembling child
Why is it thus with me?

There is a longing in my heart—
Did Jesus put it there?
If so, then one day I will rise
The joys of heav'n to share!

Yes, there is hope—I live in hope
Of endless life above,
Not for the works that I have done
But based on God's great love.

May hope burn brighter day by day
And never, never cease,
Till its fruition brings us to
An everlasting peace.

Our Need of Christ

It is in Christ we stand or fall
And from Him all our strength must come,
And of the things we need the most
He is the substance and the sum.

We could not draw another breath
If He withdrew His providence:
Our all in all resides in Him
And He alone is our defense.

Our strongest efforts all would fail
Should He withhold His prosp'ring hand;
How sob'ring is the awesome truth
That all is under His command.

How vain for men to vaunt themselves
Who are but lowly ash and dust!
Their vap'rous lives will soon expire
Along with vanities they trust.

No man has cause to brag or boast,
Tis God who gives us our success:
We cannot save our souls from hell,
It is by grace and nothing less.

Our need of Christ defies the mind
Of feeble man to comprehend,
And how amazing is His love
That He to us would condescend.

O may we praise Him ev'ry hour
And live prostrate at His dear feet,
In hope that through His precious blood
We shall in glory one day meet.

The God I Serve

Some preach a god who tries and fails
But that is not *my* God!
The God I serve doth rule and reign
According to His word.

The God I serve performs His will
And none can stay His hand!
I will not serve a puny god
Whose purpose cannot stand.

Some say He *wants* to save all men
But this He has not done;
I'll have no such a failure god,
I might as well have none.

The God I serve has sent His Son
To cleanse His fallen bride;
And when at last time is no more
She'll be found by His side.

Her body will be perfect there,
No member will be lost;
For none can lay a charge to her,
Her husband paid the cost.

This is the sovereign God I serve,
All others I reject;
Away with gods who try and fail!
Such gods I can't respect.

The God I serve can never fail
And ne'er can be cast down;
O when He comes again may I
In righteous paths be found!

The Empty Tomb

Come see the place where Jesus lay,
He is not there, He rose!
He could not in that cold tomb stay,
He overcame His foes.

Hard-hearted Jews against Him cried,
"Let Him be crucified!"
And though no fault was found in Him
They would not be denied.

They nailed Him to a Roman cross,
Exulting in their deed,
Believing they had put an end
Unto the Holy Seed.

The darkness of that dreadful hour
Bespoke of heaven's frown,
While blood that paid redemption's price
Was trampled on the ground.

Saints laid Him in a borrowed tomb,
Men sealed it sure, they thought,
But though they tried to keep Him in
Their efforts went for naught.

The empty tomb doth volumes speak;
It shouts, "The work was done!"
It says the Father was well pleased
With His beloved Son.

Because He lives, His people live;
They died and rose, with Him;
Because He conquered death and hell
These shall not conquer them.

The empty tomb! The empty tomb!
The thought, what comfort gives!
Christ rose triumphant in our room;
He rules! He reigns! He lives!

Only the Grace of God

What cleared the darkness from these eyes of mine?
Only the grace of God;
That I might see and receive things Divine;
Only the grace of God —
Only the grace of God.
What cleared the darkness from these eyes of mine?
Only the grace of God.

What gave me tears for my wayward misdeeds?
Only the grace of God.
What was the source of my innermost needs?
Only the grace of God —
Only the grace of God.
What gave me tears for my wayward misdeeds?
Only the grace of God.

What will at last house me safely above?
Only the grace of God.
Where I forever shall bask in His love?
Only the grace of God —
Only the grace of God.
What will at last house me safely above?
Only the grace of God.

An Awakened Sinner's Prayer

Dear Lord, I am a lowly wretch,
By nature I am vile.
How can a feeble worm like me
Be called Thy precious child?

It is alone by Thy rich grace
If I am saved at all;
No power on earth apart from Christ
Could save me from the fall.

Our righteousness, like filthy rags,
Is odious to Thee;
When brought as payment for our sins
And made our only plea.

I have no righteousness to plead
Except that given me
By imputation from Thy hand…
All glory unto Thee!

The world says sinners, dead in sin,
Must let Thee in their heart,
But wicked men despise Thy name
And wish Thee to depart.

My heart belongs to Thee, dear Lord,
'Tis under Thy control;
Thou art the Potter—I'm the clay—
Have mercy on my soul.

I cannot boast of anything
My feeble hands have wrought
But if by grace I've been redeemed
My battle has been fought.

My home in heav'n has been secured
By Christ upon the cross,
And none of those for whom He died
Can in the end be lost.

I serve Him now because of love;
I cannot earn His grace;
In gratitude I praise His name
And meekly fill my place.

E'er I Sought the Lord
Thy grace appeared to me, dear Lord,
When I was dead in sin.
I wished not for Thy grace before
My soul was bom again.

T'was not for me to make the move—
I had no life within;
It took a pow'r I did not have
To save me from my sin.

Thy love was placed within my heart,
A glorious change was wrought;
Before I knew, I had new life
Exceeding human thought!

I would not e'er have sought Thy face
If Thou hadst ne'er reached down
I would have lived and died in sin
And perished 'neath Thy frown.

How could I ever thank Thee, Lord?
No merit can I claim.
But for eternity I hope
To glorify Thy name.

All praise to Thee I shall ascribe:
If saved I'm saved by grace
And through that grace I hope at last
To see Thee face to face.

The Love of God
The love of God for His elect
Can never be expressed,
And those on whom it is bestowed
Eternally are blest.

The love of God did ne'er begin
And neither shall it end;
And hence the love He has today
Is as it's always been.

It is an everlasting love
It cannot be withdrawn;
God never shall deny Himself
Nor one of His disown.

The love of God, how sweet it sounds
To those with ears to hear;
'Tis shed abroad within their hearts
And daily grows more dear.

It melts the hard and stony hearts
Of all on whom 'tis shed
And turns them from their rebel ways
As by it they are led.

The love of God! how precious 'tis
To be by it controlled;
And have it flow from breast to breast
Among His chosen fold.

Eternally this love shall last
In heaven's endless bliss
And saints shall ever praise the Lord
For giving love like this.

God's Eternal Love
The love with which God loves His own
Can never from them be withdrawn... *
Such separation cannot be
For none can frustrate God's decree
*Rom. 8:28-39

He cannot change nor vacillate
And thus His love cannot abate;*
His love for His elect is sure
Eternally it shall endure.
*Jer. 31:3

His is an all-consuming love
Thus hear Him say, "My love, my dove"; *
Love so amazing, so divine
Exceeds the grasp of mortal minds.
*S.S. 5:2

What wondrous love that Christ should die*
God's justice thus to satisfy,
That His dear chosen might go free
And heaven's glories some day see!
*Rom. 5:8

That He to earth would condescend
For such a grand and noble end
Bespeaks a love that can't be told*
T'would take forever to unfold.
*2 Cor. 9:15

Dear saints, may we always adore
And love our Saviour more and more;
Think oft of Him and His great love*
And set our heart on things above.
*Col. 3:2

The Work of Christ
Christ's death was no experiment
To see what He could do;
His was an efficacious death
The end of which He knew.

It put away the sins of all
For whom His blood was shed;
And saved His people from their sins
Just as the angel said.

He did not waste a single word
Nor shed His blood in vain;
His mission was the work of God—
For sinners He was slain.

He satisfied God's holy law
In each minute detail;
And in the work He came to do
He did not one time fail.

He overcame the greatest foe
With ne'er a hint of fault;
And set forth lessons great and true
In everything He taught.

His sacrifice upon the cross
Was pleasing in God's sight,
Because it was a perfect work
Wrought by His power and might.

God's Wondrous Works

There has to be a God on high
To rule the sea, the earth and sky.

This world is not by random chance
Or by some mindless happenstance.

Created t'was by God's great power
The mountains and the tiny flower.

It all was made by His own hand
By sheer omnipotent command.

He simply spoke and it was done,
He made all things where there was none.

How wondrously were all things made
And on a grand foundation laid.

Of dust He made a living man
From whence sprang forth a numerous clan.

And from this host He calls His own
Whom He had long before foreknown.

He sent His Son to die for them
And all these sheep shall come to Him.

In time He quickens them from sin
And puts a higher life within.

And thus their Lord they dearly love
And hope to live with Him above.

His Holy Spirit dwells within
Which makes them loathe their ev'ry sin.

At last with Christ they'll rise and fly
To everlasting peace on High.

Forever there to shout and sing
Eternal praises to their King.

Mercy

O, what mercies Thou hast showered
On my soul, O Gracious Lord,
And what pleasure, joy and blessing
All these mercies do afford!

Our redemption and salvation
Stem from Thy rich grace alone;
Only blood shed with compassion
Could our wretched sins atone.

Human merit could not help us,
Only mercy would suffice;
Grace has no concord with merit,
Christ alone has paid the price.

Grace and works cannot be partners
In procuring life divine;
"Not of works" is Paul's assertion;
All the glory, Lord, is Thine.

Creature righteousness is useless
Where redemption is concerned;
Without mercy there is justice
And a wrath that can't be turned.

Free and undeserved compassion—
Mercy graciously bestowed
Is the only hope for sinners
To reach heaven's blest abode.

None can claim the smallest parcel
Of a justifying cure,
Other than the blood of Jesus
And His mercy rich and pure.

Romans 8:35-39

Who shall sever us, Dear Savior
From thy love so kind and true?
Not the worst of tribulation
Nor the worst than man can do!

Not distress nor persecution
Nor a dearth of any kind;
Not the worst of destitution
Can Thy love restrict or bind.

Not the sharpest sword or peril
Can e'er turn Thy love away:
Tho' like sheep bound for the slaughter
Thou wilt always with us stay.

We are more than victors through Thee
Who hast loved us without end;
And we're verily persuaded
Thou wilt always be our Friend.

Neither death, nor life, nor angels
Can e'er cause Thy love to fail,
Nor the greatest worldly powers
Triumph o'er Thee or prevail.

Neither present things nor future
Nor vile dungeons e'er so deep;
Neither heights nor other creature
Can from saints Thy mercy keep.

This great gift of God in Jesus
Is secured in heav'n above,
There can be no separation
'Twixt the saints and His great love.

Musings on Eternal Things

Of Father, Son, and Holy Ghost
Let ev'ry quickened sinner boast;
God's mind, God's will, and God's decree
Combine to set the sinner free.

To Him the glory all belongs
Both in our sermons and our songs;
His word should be our daily bread
And by it thus we should be led.

To our Dear Lord all glory give
For it is He by whom we live;
Our ev'ry breath to Him we owe
And from His hand all blessings flow.

Eternal purpose, firm, secure,
Makes ev'ry promise always sure;
God cannot fail nor be cast down—
No weakness can in Him be found.

He always knows man's ev'ry thought
And brings each evil scheme to naught;
No deed by Him can go unseen
However vile, or vain, or mean.

In heav'n His grace will all unfold
As wordless beauties we behold
And there, eternal joys will flow
Such as we never knew below.

Eternal treasures will appear
And to our minds all will be clear,
Great depths that from us were concealed
Will there most sweetly be revealed.

By Grace Alone

The Lord, by grace, has saved His sheep—
—His great elected host—
And being saved by grace alone
They have no grounds to boast. *
*Matt 1:21—Eph 1:4—Eph 2:8-9

For if it be by grace alone
Then works can have no place;
And if it be by man's own works
It cannot be by grace. *
*Rom 11:6

The matter of eternal life
Lies solely with the Lord.
'Tis "not by works of righteousness," *
So says His Inspired Word.
*Titus 3:5

He gives His people works to do,
But not to get to heaven;
These rather honor God because
He has their sins forgiven. *
*Titus 3:7-8

Each heir of grace shall live with Him
Without the loss of one. *
Redemption is a finished work
Of God's beloved Son. *
*John 6:37-39—John 17:4—John 19:30

The Security of the Saints
The Lord will not cast off His people
He loved from eternity past;
He knows they are fickle and feeble,
But His blessed word is steadfast.

He chose them in Christ their Redeemer
Before this vast world was begun;
And covenant love doth sustain them
For His blessed will must be done.

His promises cannot be broken,
His oath must eternally stand;
And thus when the last words are spoken
The saints will be at His right hand.

Oh, Bless His Holy Name!
No word or deed e'er said or done
Could ever cause the Blessed One
To love a goat or hate a son;
Oh, praise His holy name!

His love has not just now begun,
Nor was the work of Christ half done,
For by His blood our peace was won;
Oh, sing His holy name!

But though He did our sin debt pay,
Our duty is not done away,
To serve Him humbly day by day;
Oh, shout His holy name!

PART 3
THE GLORY OF CHRIST

Chief Among Ten Thousand
In darkest hours of pain and grief
A view of Jesus gives us light;
Among ten thousand He is Chief—
Who turns to day our blackest night.

O let us not then yield to fear,
Though we in thickest darkness dwell,
For He, our King, is ever near
To quench the pow'r of death and hell.

Our Security
Where Jesus is I long to be;
In my distress to Him I flee;
I find in Him security,
His mercies flowing large and free.

What greater peace could we obtain?
What greater joy? what greater gain?
Our chief desire, our highest aim—
Let heav'n and earth extol His name!

Christ Revealed
Our God in His majestic might
By speaking, did create the light,
The world and all that therein lies,
The mountains and the painted skies.

And He who first commanded light
Brings darkened souls from nature's night,
Reveals the glory of His grace
In dear Messiah's lovely face.[1]

A Mighty Savior Needed
The Lord is my Redeemer,
I want, and need, no other:
He is my constant Helper,
My Friend and Elder Brother.

He blesses me in sorrows,
He comforts me when grieving,
And even when I'm sleeping
His bounties I'm receiving.

All those who know their weakness
And loathe their own behavior,
Desire a Mighty Conqueror,
A wise and sovereign Savior.

---

[1] See 2 Corinthians 4:6.

No Other Name Like Jesus

No earthly Monarch, small or great
Was e'er so great as Jesus.
No President or head of state
E'er reigned so well as Jesus.

No name has e'er been half so sweet;
How often doth it please us!
The name in which we often meet,
The blessed name of Jesus.

O may the beauty of that name
Oft' come with pow'r and seize us;
That name above all other names,
The precious name of Jesus.

⁂

God With Us

Isaiah prophesied of Christ
And did His name discuss;
Emmanuel, interpreted,
Means He is "God with us."

We look with wonder and admire
The Remedy for sin;
The Deity takes human flesh
And dwells with sinful men.

O comfort sweet! O joy divine!
No mortal tongue can tell
The mystery of godliness,
That He with men should dwell.

⁂

He Is, Was, And Is To Come

Christ is the great I AM who "is"
And ever "is" the same;
He "is" true God—He "is" true man
And *reverend* "is" *His* name.

He is the Mighty One who "was"
From all eternity,
And thus "was" God, and "was" with God
In His great Deity.

He is the One who "is to come,"
And sure as He is true,
He "is to come" and get His bride
When earth and time are through.

A Precious Friend

Weary souls may flee to Jesus
Heavy laden though they be;
He will give them rest from labor...
What a precious friend is He!

They will find His yoke is easy
When compared with yokes of men;
He who notes the fall of sparrows
Is thine only Perfect Friend.

Learn of Him ye heavy laden
He who knows thy ev'ry need;
He'll not leave thee nor forsake thee,
For He is thy Friend indeed.

Jesus, Blessed Jesus[2]

My dear Jesus, blessed Jesus;
What a grand and gracious theme!
Oh, the precious name of Jesus;
What a bright and brilliant beam!
Oh, my Jesus, dearest Jesus;
How I love to hear the sound!
Thou whose name is filled with music,
May I in Thy love be found.

Precious Jesus, fairest Jesus;
May I love Thee as I should.
Thou art altogether lovely;
Thou art altogether good.
Oh, sweet Jesus, wondrous Jesus;
What great works Thy hands have wrought!
What great things for wretched sinners!
Oh, how precious is the thought!

Oh, Thou gracious loving Jesus!
Would'st Thou raise me to Thy feet?
So that in such hallowed posture,
Thy dear name I might repeat.
Jesus, Jesus, lovely Jesus,
I would dwell before Thy throne;
Praying, praising, seeking, finding;
Ever humbly pressing on.

Oh dear Jesus! My Lord Jesus,
How I love to speak Thy name!
Thou art lovely on our mountains,

---

[2] Copyright □ 1983 by Old School Hymnal Co., Inc. and published as No. 513 in *Old School Hymnal, Eleventh Edition*. Used by permission.

In our valleys You're the same.
Precious Jesus, my dear Savior;
Thou Thy Father's darling Son;
How we hope one day to see Thee!
When our race down here is run.

Closer Than a Brother
Closer than a brother is Jesus to me,
He still abides faithful when all others flee.
He never will leave me, nor will He forsake,
This precious relation He never will break.

Friendships of earth are oft fickle and vain,
But Christ is a Friend who will ever remain.
He is not capricious and never will change,
I would not with any this friendship exchange.

Oh may I cling closely to this precious One,
This wonderful Brother, and God's Holy Son,
And may this assurance my joy ever be—
Closer than a Brother is Jesus to me.

Christ Showed His Power
Our Lord changed water into wine
And gave new vision to the blind;
He healed the sick, He raised the dead,
And multiplied the fish and bread.

He walked on water, stilled the sea,
And set poor weeping sinners free;
He showed His pow'r on ev'ry hand,
His full control on sea and land.

He opened eyes that ne'er had seen
And made the vilest sinner clean.
How blest are we His truth to see,
And His beloved child to be!

~~~

A Never-Dying Friend[3]
Jesus — a never-dying Friend
"As in the ancient days";
A covert from the tempest and
A Priest who for us prays;

A mighty King who condescends
To paupers such as we,
A Captain who directs our bark
Across life's treach'rous sea;

A Ready Scribe whose ev'ry word
Is such a priceless gem;
A wise and trusted Counselor
Who lets us sup with Him.

Our great Example, thus He is
The pattern for our feet;
An only Daysman in whose name
Mercy and truth did meet.

"Emmanuel" or "God with us";
His people rest in Him,
For He their blessed Savior is,
He gave His life for them.

---

[3] Previously published in *The Pathway of Truth*, May 1992. Used by permission.

But though He died, He rose again,
No more to bleed or die,
And will return to raise them too,
To blissful realms on high.

None but Christ

Who among the sons of men
Possesses Deity?
Which of them can raise the dead
And calm the raging sea?
Only one, and that is Christ,
Both God and man is He.

Who among the sons of men
Knows ev'ry thought and deed?
Who can call a chosen race
And meet their ev'ry need?
None but Christ, who by His grace
Doth for them intercede.

Who among the sons of men
Can melt the heart of stone,
Bring a sinner to his knees
And claim him as his own?
None but Christ can do such deeds!
What power He has shown!

Who among the sons of men
Can rise up from the tomb?
Who can take his flight to heav'n
And fill that upper room?
None but Christ, in His own pow'r
Can there a place resume.

Who among the sons of men
Can come again some day,
Raise his people from the grave
And waft them all away?
None but Christ, O may we sing.
And praise His name for aye!

Thinking of Christ
I love to think of Christ my Lord
Who came and died for sin.
Such pain as that which He endured
We cannot comprehend.

I love the words, and what they mean,
"Imputed righteousness!"
His perfect life, esteemed as mine!
He doth so richly bless.

We know but little of His grief;
Such lowly mortals, we!
How One so great could die for us
We can but dimly see.

We stood as criminals condemned,
And He our Sacrifice;
Naught but His blood could satisfy
Redemption's awful price.

He gave His life for all His sheep,
The world of His dear sons;
'Tis they alone who love His name,
They are His chosen ones.

The Father laid on Him the sins
Of ev'ry heir of grace;
He thus became their surety
And freely took their place.

The sins that would have doomed their souls
He bore on Calv'ry's cross,
And since He put their sins away
They never can be lost.

I love to think of Christ my Lord,
He is my all in all;
O may we serve Him well while we
Await His final call.

⁘

Precious is our Rock of Ages
Precious is our Rock of Ages,
He who is our lively stone;
Precious is our living Savior
While we trust in Him alone.

Precious when by faith we see Him
As He died on Calvary;
Made an end of our transgression.
Paid the debt and set us free.

Precious as our loving brother,
As our Counselor and Friend;
As our light and intercessor
He will guide us to the end.

Precious as our Priest and Prophet
To instruct us in the way,
By His virtue, grace and mercy
Gives us strength from day to day.

How I long to meet this Savior
And to see Him face to face!
And to tell that precious story
How He saved me by His grace.

No Fault in Him

Jesus Christ, our precious Savior,
Dwelt a season here on earth,
Ne'er partaking in the evil
Nor in foolishness and mirth,
For there was no fault in Him!

He was always good and gracious
But the world despised Him still,
For He would not seek their favor
But He sought His Father's will,
For there was no fault in Him!

As a sweet lamb to the slaughter
He by wicked hands was led;
And His sorrow turned more bitter
As His friends before Him fled,
But there was no fault in Him!

He was brought before vile rulers
On false charges—nothing more—
And received no form of justice
But was slandered as before;
Yet there was no fault in Him!

Wicked Pilate sought to free Him
But all justice was denied;
To the throng's demand he yielded—
"Let this man be crucified!"
But he found no fault in Him!

97

They tore His flesh by scourging Him
And stripped away His clothing,
And as they mocked Him heartlessly,
They spat upon Him with loathing:
But there was no fault in Him!

Thus for sin He died in anguish—
Sins that He did not commit;
To deliver saints from suff'ring
In the never-ending pit,
For there was no fault in Him!

Let us praise His name forever
For His purity and grace,
For the hope that we shall see Him
And shall look upon His face:
For there is no fault in Him!

<hr>

I Love the Name of Jesus

I love the name of Jesus
Above all names it stands,
The pow'r and grace of Jesus
All love and praise demands.

In Him is our salvation
And in no other name;
Though friends may often fail us
He e'er remains the same.

I love the name of Jesus;
It cheers my fainting heart
When of His grace and favor
I'm blessed to feel a part.

What joy it gives His children
To feel they are His own;
What condescending mercy
When love so great is shown!

I love the name of Jesus,
Its sweetness rings with cheer;
T'was so decreed in heaven
For He's the Saviour dear.

He saves His precious children
Without the loss of one;
In all His words and workings
His Father's will was done.

I love the name of Jesus,
The sweetest name I know,
My only hope of heaven
Or peace while here below;

My soul is firm in Jesus
Preserved in cov'nant love,
Awaiting His returning
To take us home above.

Christ is My Everything

My soul's most pure delight
Is found in Christ my King
He is my life, my Way, my All,
He is my Everything!

He is my only Hope;
Of Him alone I sing;
He is my Strength in joy or pain,
He is my Everything!

Upon His name I call
To Him my grief's I bring;
And He has been a Faithful Friend;
He is my Everything!

To Him I often flee,
To Him I daily cling,
And He has never let me down;
He is my Everything!

He died upon the cross,
Salvation thus to bring
To ev'ry heir of grace divine,
He is my Everything!

He rose up from the grave
And took away death's sting,
And in His righteousness I trust,
He is my Everything!

When saints arise from death
The halls of heav'n will ring
As with one voice they all proclaim
"He is our Everything!"

Jesus Christ Our Savior

Jesus Christ our Savior
Is a friend indeed...
He has borne our sorrows
And He knows our need.

He's the Friend of Sinners,
Prince of life and peace,
Well of living waters,
Streams that never cease.

Jesus is our Brother,
Counselor and King,
Prophet, Priest and Teacher,
Let His praises ring.

He's the Rose of Sharon,
Bright and morning star,
Lily of the valley,
Dayspring from afar.

Jesus is our Shepherd,
Gentle, meek and mild,
Everlasting Father,
Harmless, undefiled.

He's the Bread of Heaven,
Meat and drink indeed;
O Thou blest Redeemer
Grant our ev'ry need.

Jesus, Lord of Glory,
Firstborn from the dead;
He's the Hope of Zion,
Lord, and Living Head.

He's the Resurrection,
God's beloved Son;
He will come and raise us!
Victory is won!

***

When I Think of Jesus
When I think of Jesus
I think of pure perfection,
Of undisturbed duration and
His infinite perception.

When I think of Jesus
I think of His great meekness,
And power that has no equal
Without a trace of weakness.

When I think of Jesus
I think of love unceasing,
Of everlasting blissfulness
And glory ne'er decreasing.

When I think of Jesus
I think of joy supernal,
Of how He died that I might live
And have a life eternal.

When I think of Jesus
I think of heaven's splendor,
Of living there in peace with Him
Where pain can never enter.

Christ is Everything to Me
1. Jesus is my all in all!
Doth my very soul enthrall
Is my life, and breath and peace
He is everything to me!

(Chorus)
He is everything to me!
More like Him I long to be
Standing like a mighty wall
He is ere my all in all!

2. Jesus is my all in all!
Whether winter, spring or fall
On the land and on the sea
He is everything to me!

(Chorus)
He is everything to me
Such a blessed Friend is He
Oft upon Him I must call
Jesus is my all in all!

3. Jesus is my all in all!
Like a mighty mountain tall
None so beautiful as He
He is everything to me!

(Chorus)
He is everything to me!
Ever is, and ere shall be
Jesus for eternity
Will be everything to me.

He Knows

Our Savior knows each deed we do
Each word we speak and if it's true;
He knows our hearts before we speak
And ev'ry blessing that we seek.

He knows our ev'ry fear and doubt
And how to drive those troubles out;
He knows the limits of our strength;
He knows our mind and what we think.

He knows when our poor heart is broke
And knows that we're a feeble folk;
He knows that we on Him rely
And without Him we soon would die.

He knows each tear before it falls,
Each saint's petition ere he calls;
He knows when we are sinking low
And just what mercies to bestow.

He knows when unkind words are said
And when our comforts all have fled;
He knows just how to make it right
And change our grief to pure delight.

He knows when persecution strikes
And lays its lash upon our backs;
He knows just how to turn the darts
And how to soothe our aching hearts.

He knows how fleeting is our breath
And knows the hour of our death;
He knows just how to make it sweet
And make us glad that hour to greet.

✦

O What Love![4]
When Jesus appears to the eyes of my soul
And I am engrossed in His love,
My heart seems to soar above all things below
'Tis as though I have wings as a dove.
O what love, glorious love, O what grace, saving grace,
O what love, O what grace, from above!

Sometimes I seem near to the portals above
And almost can see through the veil;
But then there are times when the Lord seems withdrawn
Yet I know that His love will not fail.

---

[4] May be sung to the tune "It Is Well With My Soul."

Love abides, love abides, E'er abides, never dies,
His great love, to my soul, never dies!

Though burdened with sin in this present evil world
Awaiting are pleasures untold;
Beyond this dark vale there is endless delight
With a glorified body and soul.
Glorified, sanctified, purified, satisfied,
Glorified, with my Lord, to abide!

When life here is ended and we fly away
To regions above earthly woes,
We'll know no more pain, and we'll shed no more tears
For the Lord will have vanquished our foes.
O what peace, perfect peace, lasting peace, joyous peace,
Wondrous peace, with the Lord, ne'er shall cease!

***

Jesus is My Savior[5]
"Jesus, Lord, we look to Thee,
Let us in Thy name agree." #62
May we sing with hearts made free,
Jesus is my Savior.

"Holy Ghost, with light divine,
Shine upon this heart of mine." #77
Let me shout this treasured line;
Jesus is my Savior.

"Jesus, Savior, pilot me,
Over life's tempestuous sea." #92
Make these words more sweet to me,
Jesus is my Savior.

---

[5] The first two lines of each stanza are taken from the numbered songs in the *Old School Hymnal, Eleventh Edition*. The verses may be sung to the tune of "Hand in Hand With Jesus" #40.

"God of love, O hear our prayer;
Kindly for Thy people care." #103
Grant thy saints these words to share,
Jesus is my Savior.

"Prince of Peace, control my will;
Bid this struggling heart be still." #105
May this thought my spirit fill,
Jesus is my Savior.

"Depth of mercy! Can there be
Mercy still reserved for me?" #328
This shall be my only plea,
Jesus is my Savior.

❦

The Rejected Stone
The Stone that the builders refused,
'Tis He that my soul doth desire;
Though falsely He oft was accused
Yet His blessed name I admire.

This great Priest-Prophet, and King-
Despised and rejected of men,
Of Him I desire most to sing
Who saved His elect from their sin.

This perfect example of love
Was hated by men without cause
And though He came down from above
They would not acknowledge His laws.

This great Prince of Peace, full of grace,
Was treated as though He were vile;
Men beat Him and spit in His face
Though in Him there never was guile.

He e'er was *with* God in Glory
And without Him nothing was made;
Thus goes the old gospel story—
He stands not in need of man's aid.

O, Let all the saints adore Him
And thusly extol Him each day;
For grace let them e'er implore Him
And all of His teachings obey.

Stone that the builders rejected!
And *King* that the world doth despise!
By Him His saints are protected
And by Him they shall yet arise.

Words Do Not Suffice

No words in all the tongues of men
Are ample to portray,
The glory of our risen Lord—
What can a mortal say?

We feeble worms of dust can ne'er
Declare truth so sublime,
In words that fully set Him forth—
No! Never here in time.

Some things are better felt than said
And words do not suffice;
But all will be revealed at last
In heaven's Paradise.

PART 4
CHRISTIAN EXPERIENCE

Growth in Grace Desired
Lord grant that we may be imbued
With humble and fervent desire,
To grow in Thy marvelous grace
And knowledge Divine to acquire;
That while on this earth we may be
More deeply devoted to Thee.

No Darkness in Christ
There is no night where Jesus is,
All darkness flees away;
Where He reveals His lovely face
No gloom or grief can stay.

He is the life of every heart
Where grace has been instilled,
And none can tread a path of gloom
While with His presence filled.

Growing Stronger
The burdens and the trials of life
Help us to stronger grow;
To trust more fully in the Lord
From whom all blessings flow.

The conflicts that obstruct our way
Sometimes are hard to bear,
But if they help us grow in grace,
We'll gladly take our share.

All is Well
When past offenses bring us low,
And Sinai's loudest thunders roar,
Then Christ our Substitute appears,
And Justice says, "I ask no more."

When sin, like mountains, bar our way,
And fears like raging billows swell,
Then Christ stands as our Advocate,
And sweetly whispers, "All is well."

Christian Experience

Our path is oft beset with sin;
With foes without and foes within.
We feel our poverty and need,
And pray that God would gently lead.
In His own time and way He hears,
And drives away our anxious fears.

A Prayer

Let me live for Thee, Dear Master;
Let my life be wholly Thine;
Sharing that which Thou hast lent me,
Never claiming ought as mine.

Let me now and then be granted
Freedom to approach Thy throne;
Let my hope be in Thy mercy
And in Thy rich grace alone.

My Gifts are Thine

Lord, what I have is not my own,
It is a gift from Thee;
The good I do originates
From grace Thou gavest me.

O may I take no credit, Lord,
For gifts within my hand
Which glorify Thy precious name
Or help my fellow man.

O may Thine anger still my tongue
If I should claim as mine
The graces Thou hast given me,
For these, O Lord, are Thine.

※

Improvement Promoted

Our trials, afflictions and burdens
Are often so heavy to bear,
But these promote our improvement
If Jesus, our Savior, is there.

His presence gives peace and comfort;
No words could begin to express.
We beg, Lord, abide Thou near us
In our heartaches and sore distress.

※

The Chief Desire

Though sin abounds within my flesh
Thy grace, Lord, doth excel,
And if in Thee I have a part
Then with my soul 'tis well.

Whom do I have in heav'n but Thee?
This world has lost its charms!
My chief desire is rest within
Thine everlasting arms.

※

Heart Affects the Face

Remember when thy day doth start
Thy count'nance will reflect thy heart,
For if thy heart in heaven be
Thy face will show a touch of glee.

We've always heard here and about
That smiles are frowns turned in-side-out.
When cares of life are pressing down
It never helps to wear a frown.

Think Upon Past Favors

May we hold fast in memory
The mercies of the past,
And strive to show our gratitude
As long as breath shall last.

Reflecting on past favors helps
To cheer us on our way,
For He who helped us in the past
Is just the same today.

Thou Art My Life

From Thee, O Lord, I cannot stay,
Though I am prone to often stray.
Thou art my life, each hour, each day;
Abide with me, I humbly pray.

Through fire and flood be Thou my Guide,
And keep me from all carnal pride.
Help me to stand, whate'er betide,
And in Thy love to e'er abide.

Heavenly Cordials

An humble walk with Christ our Lord
Is worth far more than gold;
A life of faith brings peace in youth
And cheers us when we're old.

The charms of earth will disappoint
And last but for a breath,
But heav'nly cordials lift our souls
And bless us ev'n in death.

To Whom Could We Go?

If we should turn from Thee, O Lord,
To Whom else could we go?
Thou hast the words of endless life;
This truth we surely know.

There is no other place to turn;
O may we faithful be!
Thru flood, thru flame, may we hold firm,
And follow only Thee.

God Will Give Strength

O, let not ye saints think it strange
When hated by worldly men;
Whiles thou art the friend of the Lord,
They are the servants of sin.

Thy godliness oft' doth expose
Their wicked, rebellious way,
And they would with haste take thy life
If God held them not at bay.

But He who hath made thee His friend
Hath also assumed thy care,
And He will give strength to endure
Whatever load thou must bear.

Revival Desired

Lord, revive by Thy rich mercy
This cold, dead, unfeeling heart;
Give fresh tokens of Thy favor,
To my soul new peace impart.

Guide my weak and stumbling footstep
That Thy grace may be enjoyed,
And in Thy delightful service
May my soul be oft employed.

"Lord, Let It Be"

Man's days upon the earth are few,
And full of trouble his life through;
This graphic truth dear Job well knew;
Exper'ence taught him it was true.

And thus we all have found it so,
For thru our trials we've come to know
That though they often bring us low,
'Tis in this way we learn and grow.

The only way we'll ever see
The riches of God's grace so free
Is from a stance of poverty;
And hence we pray, "Lord, let it be."

Love for Christ and His Cause

Dear Lord, I love Thy precious Cause,
If I be not deceived.
What priceless faith! What saving truth,
By grace I have received!

The inner knowledge of Thy Word
Doth save me day by day;
It helps me face with confidence
The trials that come my way.

I would not with the world exchange
Thy truth for all its toys;
Its fading pleasures can't compare
With heaven's endless joys.

A Constant Need

Dear Lord, I feel my need of Thee,
A constant, daily, hourly need;
Quench not this little smoking flax,
Break not this bruised and trembling reed.

My enemies are great, dear Lord,
I dare not face them without Thee:
Bear Thou me up through fire and flood
And give me final victory.

He Sees Our Tears
Our Savior sees each tear we shed
And knows the pain thereof;
For He can sweetly empathize
And succour with His love.

He took a part of flesh and blood,
Like us, except for sin;
And thus has suffered in our stead
And borne our griefs within.

He is a Priest who can be touched
With things that cause us grief;
He knows just how to sooth our pain
And give us sweet relief.

❧

Jeremiah 12:5, or "Be Not Soon Wearied"
If running with the footmen
Hath wearied thee, dear one,
Canst thou contend with horses
When with them thou dost run?

And if thou art now wearied
While dwelling still in peace,
Beware of Jordan's swelling
When sorrows shall increase.

If thou be so soon wearied
How canst thou stand the test?
Compared with what *could* face thee
Thy soul is now at rest.

❧

A Blessed Place

O what a blessed place to be!
A blessed place indeed!
To lie prostrate at Jesus' feet
With naught of self to plead.

To realize our utter ruin
Apart from sov'reign love,
And know that only through His grace
Shall any rest above.

O help us, Lord, to fill this place
And always give our best,
Until we reach a better place,
A place of endless rest.

True Humility

The crowning virtue of the saint
Is true humility;
It draws him to the highest ground
Yet keeps him on his knee.

True meekness is a priceless grace;
It is a Christ-like trait;
It lays the mighty in the dust
And makes the lowly great.

It never pleads for its own praise
Nor seeks another's fall;
It e'er exalts the Savior's name
And crowns Him Lord of all.

O Thou Ingratitude, Begone

Ingratitude, ingratitude:
O, what an ugly sin!
And yet how common is this vice
Ev'n in the best of men.

How blest we are! No tongue can tell!
Ingratitude, depart!
Let thoughtlessness and thanklessness
Remove from ev'ry heart!

Help us to be more grateful, Lord,
Forgetting not to pray;
Acknowledging with thankful hearts
The blessings of each day.

Desire for God's Help

Forgive, O Lord, the wayward step,
The careless thought or deed;
Be Thou our constant Friend and Help
In ev'ry hour of need.

Attend us when we bow in prayer,
Restore us when we fall;
In ev'ry step along life's way
Be Thou our All in All.

Uphold us when we're tempted sore
And troubles bend us low.
When grief lies heavy at our door
More grace on us bestow.

No Reason for Alarm

If God doth o'er our persons watch
And keep us safe from harm,
Then all is well and there shall be
No reason for alarm.

His promise is that He doth keep
His people by His pow'r;
He watches o'er them when they sleep
And ev'ry waking hour.

Though all the pow'rs of hell engage
To ruin us at last,
The love of God shall be our shield,
'Til all the storms are past.

The Prayer of Faith

Oft' times when we attempt to pray,
Desiring to be blest,
We speak as though we think the Lord
Can grant no large request.

Our faith sometimes is tinged with doubt
But He is faithful still;
He hears the prayers of those who pray
According to His will.

Great things may be expected from
A God so great as He;
He'll ne'er deny the prayer of faith,
Whatever it may be.

Wealth Untold
The smallest grain of heav'nly grace
Is worth far more than gold,
And O how grand is life divine!
Its value can't be told.

Contentment with true godliness
Is gain beyond compare;
How rich are those who look above
And long to enter there!

How precious is each Bible truth
When seen through quickened eyes!
And this revives our hope of heav'n
Where greater treasure lies.

The Lord is There
A mother may forget her child,
Who on her bosom lay;
But God will not forget His saints
Nor cast their souls away.

Tho' friends may often let us down
And cause our hearts to bleed,
The Lord is ever by our side
Supplying ev'ry need.

Thru fire and flood the Lord is there,
In air, on sea, or land;
Where'er we go, whate'er we do,
He holds us in His hand.

Sufficient Grace—2 Cor. 12:9
Like Paul of old we have our thorns
And from them wish that we were free;
But that same word applies to us
"Sufficient is my grace for thee."

Oft-times our way is dark and drear
And there's but one place we can flee;
We cling like drowning men to this:
"Sufficient is my grace for thee."

In all the trials through which we pass,
May this our constant comfort be,
That we can claim these precious words,
"Sufficient is my grace for thee."

Our Needy State
How helpless we poor mortals are!
By grace alone we stand.
Each heartbeat is a gift from God—
A cordial from His hand.

We could not draw another breath
If He did not provide;
We could not face another foe
Without Him by our side.

O may we ever mindful be
Of our poor, needy frame,
And always look to Him for strength
And glorify His name.

Don't Borrow From Tomorrow

We know not what a day may bring,
It may bring pain or sorrow;
It is not wise to search for grief
Nor borrow from tomorrow.

Sufficient is the evil which
Each passing day doth bring us,
We should not fret o'er what *might* be
Nor let such worries sting us.

Imagined griefs may never come,
Our lives are so uncertain;
Just face your days one at a time,
Don't look behind their curtain.

We Need the Lord

Sometimes we find our courage low
And faith burns with the faintest glow;
'Tis at such times we're made to know
Just how we need the Lord.

Each day our footsteps grow more slow,
The signs of age more plainly show,
And this reminds us as we go
How much we need the Lord.

God's people face a common foe
While trav'ling thru this world below,
And life's experience makes them know
They'll always need the Lord.

He'll Stand With You
If you should have to stand alone
In order to be strong and true,
Remember, God is on His throne,
And He will always stand with you.

Sometimes in faithfulness to Him
You must oppose what others do;
But you may rest assured when right
That He will ever stand with you.

And when you face the foe called *death*,
Your final struggle almost through,
Take courage, child, and rest assured
That He'll be standing there with you.

I Cannot Stand Alone
For ev'ry breath, O Lord, most High,
I look alone to Thee;
For strength I must on Thee rely,
For grace to Thee I flee.

I know I cannot stand alone,
I dare not even try;
If Thou should'st leave me on my own
I'd quickly fade and die.

O stay, dear Lord, close to my heart,
I am so weak and frail;
And when I must from earth depart
Let not my courage fail.

In His Care

O what a dark and bitter path
We oft-times must traverse!
But matters not how bad things are,
They always could be worse.

God will not put more of a load
On us than we can bear;
And even when it seems He's gone
We're in His loving care.

Christ will not let His children go
For whom He bled and died;
And in their most distressing hours
He's there, close by their side.

Cast Thy Care Upon The Lord

O pilgrim friend, and child of God,
Bowed down with earthly woes,
Tho' others may not understand
There is a Friend who knows.

Cast all thy care upon the Lord—
To Him thy troubles take;
Remember that He cares for you
And never will forsake.

Tho' pain may sometimes bring thee low,
Yea, almost to despair,
Ev'n in these very-worst of times
Thy heav'nly Friend is there.

A Morning Prayer

O Gracious Father, wise and true,
Bestow Thy mercies large and free,
And may whate'er we say and do
Extol thy name and honor Thee.

Throughout this day may we hold fast
To Thy inerrant, inspired word,
And may our cares on Thee be cast
And no ill word from us be heard.

And then at close of day may we
Beseech Thy watch care o'er our bed,
And ask for grace to follow Thee
Thru all the days that lie ahead.

Consider the Lilies

Consider the lilies how they grow —
They do not toil, they do not spin;
Consider their clothing all aglow —
They have a wise and wondrous Friend.

Consider the lilies and reflect
Upon the artistry of God;
Consider the picture they project
And how they speak His name abroad.

Consider the lilies and believe
Thy God will always care for thee;
Consider the bounties we receive
And know that thus t'will ever be.

Deep in my Heart[1]

Oh Lord my God, my soul doth long for Thee!
Deep in my heart Thy face I long to see;
I wish to feel Thy blessed presence near
And long for freedom from this earthly sphere.

Lord, wouldst Thou send refreshing to my soul
For I so often feel so dead and cold;
Wouldst Thou revive me and renew my zeal
For I so much desire Thy love to feel.

Draw me, O Savior, and I'll fly to Thee!
'Tis in Thy bosom that I long to be;
And when my eyelids close in death may I
Find what a joy it is in Thee to die.

To Thee I Fly

Oh Lord, my God, to Thee I fly
When storms assail and foes decry;
In Thee I find the binding tie
Betwixt my soul and things on high.

But matters not how hard I try,
I often feel quite cold and dry;
So far from Thee I feel to be
And often breathe the mourner's sigh.

O help me e'er to Thee draw nigh
And to my soul Thy truth apply;
Now guide me with Thy watchful eye
And take me to Thee when I die.

---

[1] May be sung to the tune "Spirit of God, Descend Upon My Heart." No. 79 in *Old School Hymnal, Eleventh Edition.*

The Chastening of the Lord
I have often felt the rod
Of a caring Father God,
Who, in love, has chastened me,
That I might more humble be.

E'vn the hidings of His face
Are an evidence of grace,
And will issue good to me,
Though just how I may not see.

He reproves me as His child
And I'm sweetly reconciled—
This appears to me a sign—
I am His and He is mine!

Only Thou
Great God, when sorrow grieves my soul
And anguish makes me groan,
Grant tokens of Thy grace and love
And make Thy presence known.

Thou art the only source of help
For sinners such as me;
No other pow'r can reach my case,
None else can hear my plea.

Thou knowest all my inner thoughts,
My greatest doubts and fears;
And only Thou canst ease my mind
And wipe away my tears.

Be Thou My Companion

Gracious Father let Thy Spirit
My Companion ever be,
As I face the daily conflicts
That attend my walk with Thee.

Go before me in the darkness;
Lead me gently through the night;
And when morning breaks around me,
Help me praise Thy name aright.

I am hast'ning swiftly onward...
Soon this mortal life shall cease;
Then, O Lord, would'st Thou receive me
To that land of endless peace.

Cast All on Christ

Whate'er thy griefs and burdens are
They may on Christ be cast;
The promise is that He will grant
Whate'er in faith we ask.

Be not so faithless, precious one
But on Him cast Thy all;
He will not fail to meet thy need
Nor spurn thy humble call.

Death may a monster now appear
But Christ removed its sting;
And soon our souls to heav'n will fly
His praises e'er to sing.

When My Way is Hard
When my way is hard
I go to God in prayer;
I cast my burdens at His feet
And strive to leave them there.

When my way is hard
I know who holds the key
To sweet relief and calm repose,
And He will hear my plea.

When my way is hard
There's nowhere else to go;
And in His arms I shall find rest
From ev'ry grievous foe.

Is It Thus With You?
Dreary are the hours that we
Dimly our dear Savior see,
Longing for a clearer view,
Tell me, is it thus with you?

Sadly do we plod along
When it seems our Lord is gone;
Then our joys are very few,
Tell me, is it thus with you?

How our hearts do ache and yearn
For the joy of His return
Our sad hearts to oft renew!
Tell me, is it thus with you?

No Matter How Distressed

Through darkest vale and blackest night
Thou, Lord, hast held our feeble hand,
To guide our feet and give us light
And lead us through this dreary land.

Sometimes in grief and sinking down,
Distressed and almost in despair,
Thy comforts have been sweetly found
While trusting in Thy faithful care.

Look ye to Him who are cast down,
No matter how distressed you be;
His mercies reach the world around
And span the earth from sea to sea.

No Sweeter Place

I'll never find a place more sweet
Than at my Dear Redeemer's feet;
'Tis there I learn, 'tis there I grow,
And triumph over every foe.

That hallowed place no man can give
Is where I long to ever live;
For Satan can't distress me there
Nor wrest me from my Savior's care.

At His dear feet I feel secure
And worldly things have no allure;
While thus I view His lovely face,
I want no other hiding place.

A Heart Right with God

Dear Lord, I know I often fail,
And am not what I ought to be;
But this one thing I humbly ask,
Oh, may my heart be right with Thee.

Oft' times I feel so dead and cold,
The flesh and spirit don't agree;
But, Lord, Thou knowest what's inside,
I hope my heart is right with Thee.

When life departs this house of clay,
I trust Thy blessed face to see;
And that will be my happy lot,
If this poor heart is right with Thee.

Small, Yet So Blest

How minuscule we mortals are
Compared to all of space!
Within this boundless universe
We fill a tiny place.

We are a speck, yet in our hearts
The Master opts to dwell;
And just how great this mystery is
No sage or poet can tell.

Our littleness compared to Him
Doth lay us at His feet,
Adoring Him and longing soon
With Him in heav'n to meet.

Inward Peace

Lord, though the storms may rage about
This mortal house of sin;
No matter what transpires without,
Give me sweet peace within.

Calmness of soul, Oh what a gift!
May that my pleasure be;
All cares Thou canst from my heart lift
And give sweet peace with Thee.

No foe without can pierce the shield
Of Thy protecting care;
To Thee my trusting heart doth yield
And I am resting there.

God's Righteous Will

We ought to seek God's holy will
And ne'er to seek our own;
The only perfect way there is,
Is His, and His alone.

He knows exactly what is right
In every single case;
And we should seek His righteous will
In everything we face.

Another way, whate'er the source,
Will surely lead astray;
Hence, let us yield our will to His
Each step along the way.

He Will Do Us Good

God may not give us all we ask,
But if not, we're still blest,
For He sees all and knows quite well
What things for us are best.

He knows the end before the start
All things to Him are plain;
No deed can take Him by surprise
Nor His great pow'r restrain.

May we be reconciled to Him
And to His holy will,
Assured that He will do us good
And all His word fulfill.

At Thy Feet

At Thy feet, Oh blessed Savior,
Let me live and let me die;
It is there I feel most happy,
May I there to Thee draw nigh.

At Thy feet I am in safety,
Satan's darts are turned away;
Darkness cannot there distress me
Nor can skies be glum and gray.

At Thy feet my soul is nourished
And 'tis there I want to live;
There I find a sweet submission,
There to Thee my all I give.

A Sweet Hope

I have a sweet assuring hope
Abiding in my breast
Of things unseen, of things divine,
Of everlasting rest.

This hope a precious blessing is,
An anchor of the soul;
It gives me consolation dear
And peacefulness untold.

It never leaves me night or day
'Tis mine each step I take;
But one day soon that hope will end
When I in heaven awake.

In Times of Trouble

In times of trouble and distress
How good it is to know,
We have a Friend who cares for us
And will compassion show.

He will not leave us nor forsake,
Our times are in His hand;
His grace will be sufficient and
Our need is His command.

No grief can ever be so great
That He cannot provide
Sweet comfort and deliverance—
Near Him let us abide.

If God be for Us

"If God be for us," who can harm us?
Who against us can succeed?
All the powers of hell oppose us
But those powers He doth impede.

If the Lord is our Protector,
We are safely in His care;
None can go beyond His fetter,
He has numbered every hair.

It is Christ who died to save us,
Who then can our souls condemn?
In His love we're bound securely
And we find our all in Him.

Our Daily Bread

"Give us this day our daily bread"
For by Thy hand, Lord, we are fed;
Help us to live as Thou hast said
And by Thy word be always led.

"Thy kingdom come, Thy will be done,"
Help us the Christian race to run;
Of worth or merit we have none
Except in Thee, God's darling Son.

The kingdom and the power are Thine;
We are the branches—Thou the Vine;
Let heav'n and earth and sea combine
To magnify Thy truth divine.

No Other Option

Feeble are my best endeavors
To exalt God's wondrous grace;
But I must put forth the effort,
Must pursue the Christian race.

There is not another option
For the humble, sincere saint;
He must ever follow Jesus
And be watchful lest he faint.

Help me Lord, to e'er be faithful
In this struggle for the right;
Till I'm carried home to glory
And embraced in endless light.

~ ∞ ~

Jesus is my Refuge

I daily meet with trouble
Along the road of life,
For there's a daily struggle
And conflicts, they are rife.

Hence oft I look toward heaven
From whence all mercy flows;
For there's a promise given
For all my griefs and woes.

Dear Jesus is my refuge
As troubles press me sore;
He always has sustained me
And will till life is o'er.

~ ∞ ~

A Fount That Ne'er Runs Dry

In Thee, dear Lord, we find our all...
Thou art our Everything;
Thy grace is all-sufficient, and
All blessings from Thee spring.

There is no lack of anything
That for our good would be,
And for all things we sinners need,
Dear Lord, we look to Thee.

An endless source of help Thou art,
A Fount that ne'er runs dry;
Thine ear is ever tuned to hear
The needy sinner's cry.

Deliverance Will Come

What cares and troubles oft distress
My unbelieving mind!
I sometimes seem so far from God,
And peace I cannot find.

I'm troubled by the gloom of night
And dwell in Baca's vale;
And sometimes hope seems almost gone
As heavenly comforts fail.

But we are taught in Holy writ
That God, in time, will save;
His Spirit will renew our hope
And give the peace we crave.

Help Me Lord

Help me, Dear Lord, to see the road
That I should daily take;
Help me to bear life's heavy load
And ne'er the truth forsake.

Help me to e'er courageous be
While fighting for the right;
That I may e'er on bended knee
Find favor in Thy sight.

Life's battles I shall surely win
If Thou art by my side;
And I'll at last be free from sin
When I am glorified!

A Longing Soul

As the copious dew of heaven
Let Thy blessings, Lord, come down;
Let compassion thus be given
And Thy mercy thus abound.

Here I bow — my soul is thirsting
For the moisture from above;
And my heart is well nigh bursting
For the tokens of Thy love.

Like a bird my mouth is open,
Longing to be kindly fed;
Thus I plead, as Thou hast spoken,
Grant to me my daily bread.

The Lord Has Promised

The Lord has promised, yes, 'tis true
That He'll supply our every need;
That He will keep us our lives through
And in the good way gently lead.

He hath besought us not to fret
About tomorrow's cares and woes;
Let *this day's* burdens first be met—
Don't try to face *tomorrow's* foes.

Go leaning on His mighty hand,
Assured that He will faithful be;
There's just a step to Glory Land—
Then, Oh, what beauties we shall see!

Very, Very Blest

He who loved me with an everlasting love
Is the same who made me love His precious name;
Put a longing in my heart for things above
And a yearning His sweet gospel to proclaim.

He prepared me from my youth to bear the cross,
That a faithful servant must with courage bear;
And He made me willing thus to bear the loss
Of a host of things for which most others care.

Never have I wished I'd gone another way,
For the path He chose for me I'm sure is best;
After many years of service I can say,
I have always been so very, very blest.

Swift and Slow

Swift to hear, slow to speak
Let me always be;
Slow to fear, swift to seek
Shelter, Lord, in Thee.

Swift to pray, slow to think
Of my burdens here;
Swift to praise, slow to sink
Into doubt and fear.

Swift to sing, slow to bring
Gloom where e'er I go;
Swift to cling, to my King,
Thus in grace to grow.

Why Should We Fear?

Why should we fear our tomorrows
Since God is so firmly in charge?
Why should we fret what *may* happen
While knowing His love is so large?

Why should we grieve o'er our losses
When nothing we have is our own?
Why should we covet more riches
When all of them soon will be gone?

Let us not live in the future
Nor linger too much in the past;
Our present distress is sufficient
And all on the Lord should be cast.

Wait on the Lord

When light seems far withdrawn from thee
And hopeful signs are hard to see,
Cease not to make thy upward plea
And wait upon the Lord.

In His own time He'll intercede
And thus supply each pressing need;
Thus to His promises give heed
And take Him at His word.

May we not grope in unbelief;
The Lord knows all our pain and grief,
And in due time will give relief
According to His word.

∽∾

Encircle Us Lord

Encircle us, Dear Lord most high,
With Thy sweet Spirit pure;
And bless us oft to Thee draw nigh
And feel in Thee secure.

O may our hearts and lives be filled
With blessings from above;
And thus be made to know and feel
The depths of Thy great love.

On thru the journey guide our way
And help us firmly stand;
As we with joy await the day
We enter Glory Land.

∽∾

By Him We Are Fed
A difficult road here we travel,
A wearisome path here we tread;
But God gives us grace for the struggle
And by His great hand we are led.

He knows all our trouble and anguish;
He knows all our grief that's ahead;
But why should we grumble and languish
While being so graciously led.

To pastures of green He has brought us
And there we've been graciously fed;
And all through His word He has taught us
We always by Him will be led.

ᷞ

Bow Down My Soul
Bow down thy soul unto the Lord,
Contrite and humble be;
Submit thyself to His great will
For this is best for thee.

Commit thy all unto His hands
For He knows what is best;
Do what He has commanded thee
And leave to Him the rest.

To Him be fully reconciled
And trust not thine own way;
Bow down to Him in everything
And praise Him, come what may.

ᷞ

My Cup Runs Over

My cup runs over when I see,
By faith, a place in heav'n for me;
O glorious thought, say, can it be
That I'm secured by heaven's decree?

My cup runs over when I view
God's lovely things, so good, so true,
As words from heaven, not a few
Refresh my soul as manna new.

My cup runs over when I feel
The tokens of His love so real;
Before His throne I humbly kneel
Confiding in His power to heal.

In All Circumstances

Through the dark places
As well as the bright
I need Thee, Lord Jesus
To guide me aright.

I'll need Thee forever,
In grief and in glee,
In all circumstances
My Savior to be.

Without Thee to help me
O where would I be?
I'll always be running
Dear Savior, to Thee.

O Peaceful Hour!
O peaceful hour, O time of cheer,
When I can feel my Savior near.
When He endues me with a sign
That I am His and He is mine!

How joyous are those days when He
Rolls back the clouds and lets me see
Some glimpses of His truth so dear
And for a time relieves my fear!

Oh how I long at last to dwell
In that bright land where all is well:
To live always in sweet accord
With all the saints and with the Lord!

My Beacon, My Compass
O Thou source of life and light
Be my Beacon through the night;
Be my compass day by day
Lest my feet should go astray.

O Thou source of grace Divine
Keep this wand'ring heart of mine;
Be my Friend when others fail
And my Help when foes assail.

O Thou everlasting Friend
Be my Comfort to the end;
Drape my dying bed with love,
Then escort my soul above.

Longing to Be Like Him

A broken and a contrite heart
Thou, Lord, wilt surely not despise;
May I in these traits share a part
For they are precious in Thine eyes.

Let me be meek in heart, Dear Lord,
And live at Thy beloved feet
With humble saints who love Thy word
And seek its treasures, pure and sweet.

O meek and lowly Lamb of God,
Help me to be what I should be;
Wherever I am called to trod
I greatly long to be like Thee.

All in Him

No fleshly wings have I
And yet sometimes I fly
As on the wings of heav'nly love
I soar to realms on high.

I cannot long rejoice
For nature pulls me down;
But grace can overcome the flesh
And make my joy abound.

I have no wealth in gold,
Yet I am rich indeed,
For, jointly, I'm an heir of Christ
And of the royal seed.

No righteousness have I
Except in Christ my King;
And for my blessings, all in Him,
His praise I'll ever sing.

Wash Me
"Purge me with hyssop,
And I shall be clean;
Wash me and I shall
Be whiter than snow."

Let me rejoice in
The truths I have seen,
And daily to Thee
May I closer grow.

Keep Me, Dear Savior
Leave me not to grope in darkness,
Else, dear Lord, I'll lose my way;
Shine Thy blessed light about me
That I may not go astray.

Keep my feeble feet from stumbling
When the Tempter lays his snares;
Overrule his vile devices
While on Thee I cast my cares.

Be not far from me, Dear Savior,
While along life's path I plod;
Thou alone can keep me safely—
Thou my life, and Thou my God.

Cast Thy Cares on Jesus
When thy way is fraught with care
And thy woes are hard to bear,
Do not sink in deep despair—
Cast thy cares on Jesus.

When great fears are realized
And thy heart is filled with sighs,
Wipe the teardrops from' thine eyes—
Cast thy cares on Jesus.

There is none so good as He,
Go to Him on bended knee;
He will ever faithful be,
Cast thy cares on Jesus.

One Moment with God
One moment in our Lord's embrace
Doth all our tears of grief erase;
One glimpse of His soul-cheering face
Doth make us sing with joy.

One word of cheer from His sweet lips
Doth ev'ry earthly joy eclipse;
His love our hearts with pleasure grips
And evil can't annoy.

One breath of Heaven's blissful clime
Will blot all troubles from our mind,
And rev'ling in this bliss sublime
Will be our full employ.

In a Strait

Upon the sea of life I'm tossed,
At times feel safe, oft times seem lost;
Sometimes I laugh, sometimes I cry;
I love to live, yet long to die.

I'm sometimes up and sometimes down,
Sometimes I smile, sometimes I frown;
I long so much my Lord to see
And from all ill to be set free.

I'm full of sin, yet sin I hate;
Like Paul of old, I'm in a strait:
I want to leave, I want to stay,
But God must have the final say.

How Blest They Are!

How richly blest God's people are
To have a Friend so great as He;
A Great Protector in the storm,
An Anchor in life's troubled sea!

How blest they are to hear His voice,
Sometimes in song, or when they pray;
Sometimes by sermon preached in pow'r,
Sometimes when sorrow clouds their way.

How blest they'll be to be caught up
By pow'r surpassing mortal thought,
At last in heav'n to praise His name
For all the wonders He hath wrought.

We Walk By Faith[2]

We walk by faith and not by sight,
Through shadows dim and darkest night;
Faith sees beyond earth's flick'ring light
To realms so lustrous, pure and bright.

By faith to us it is revealed
That by the stripes of Christ we're healed;
That His decrees are ne'r repealed,
And in His love the saints are sealed.

It is by faith we understand
The worlds were made by His command,
And are sustained just as He planned,
For all His counsel firmly stands.

Faith helps us dry the troubled tear
For we can see our help is near,
And when we're faced with doubts and fear,
Faith makes these mountains disappear.

By faith the martyrs faced the flame
And ev'n in death they praised God's name;
And thus for Him they suffered shame
And did His faithfulness proclaim.

O may we stand as firm as they
If persecuted in this way;
And prove that Satan cannot stay
That faith which none can take away.

Faith lets us look within the veil
To see a God who cannot fail;
And though we are so weak and frail,
In faith we shall at last prevail.

---

[2] Previously published in the *Baptist Witness*, July 1986. Used by permission.

By faith the world we shall defeat
And vict'ry will indeed be sweet;
And when at last in heav'n we meet,
Our faith will end at Jesus' feet.

The Assurance of Faith[3]

What calm repose is bred by faith
Within the hearts of God's elect!
It gives assurance that their Lord
Will surely guide, guard and protect.

It helps them to endure the trials
Which dot their path from day to day;
And gives a holy confidence
That God will hear them when they pray.

It is to ev'ry quickened soul
What eyes are to this mortal frame;
It looks within the realm of bliss
And glories in the Savior's name.

It lets the saints look fondly toward
The day when Christ returns to earth;
It gives a foretaste of His love
And makes them realize its worth.

---

[3] Previously published in *The Pathway of Truth*, October 1991. Used by permission.

The Twenty-Third Psalm[4]
The Lord my loving Shepherd is,
Supplying all my needs;
In pastures green He makes me lie
And by still waters leads.

Restores my soul and gently guides
In paths of righteousness;
Yea, though I walk thru shades of death
This valley He will bless.

No fear of evil shall invade
While thru its gloom I stroll;
For Thou art with me and I know
Thy rod and staff console.

Before me Thou hast set a feast
While in the midst of foes;
Anointed is my head with oil,
My cup with joy o'er-flows.

Thy goodness surely shall abide
With me throughout my days;
And in Thy house, O gracious Lord,
I'll surely dwell always.

---

[4] Previously published in *The Pathway of Truth*, June 1992. Used by permission.

Psalm 130
Out of the depths, O Lord my God,
My soul hath cried to Thee;
O hear my voice,—Lord lend Thine ear,
And grant a sinner's plea.

If Thou, O Lord, should mark our sins,
And keep them close at hand;
We all, alas, would be condemned,
And none of us could stand.

With Thee there is forgiveness, Lord,
That feared Thou mayest be;
My hope is in Thy precious word;
My soul doth wait for Thee.

More than the watchers for the morn,
For Thee my soul doth wait;
More than the lovers of its dawn,
Upon their shadowed pate.

Redemption, Lord, with Thee is great;
Let Israel hope in Thee;
And with Thee, too, is mercy sweet,
And love beyond degree.

Thou, Lord, shalt all Thy saints redeem
From all their guilt and sin;
O may we praise Thy precious name,
Forevermore,—Amen!

I'd Rather Walk With Jesus

If all the world were made of gold
And every ounce of it were mine,
I'd give it all for one sweet view
Of Him who made the sun to shine.

I'd rather live in poverty
And walk with Jesus day by day,
Than live in temp'ral luxury
And then at last be cast away.

The wealth of earth will soon dissolve;
It is not ours beyond the grave;
It cannot purchase happiness
Nor has it pow'r our souls to save.

O may God's kingdom occupy
Our chief allegiance and concern;
And may we seek His righteousness
Until our blessed Lord's return.

❦

Protect Me Lord

Be Thou my compass, gracious Lord,
Through life's tumultuous sea;
Protect me from its treach'rous shoals,
And bind my soul to Thee.

Help me a steady course to steer,
And each encumbrance shed,
That I be not borne down with griefs
Of fearsome doubt and dread.

Thou art the Captain, wise and just,
Of my salvation sure;
Through Thy sustaining grace alone
Shall I, through faith, endure.

When my weak heart is frightened by
The boist'rous waves of sin,
Sustain me with fresh streams of grace
And give me peace within.

The tossing billows can't surpass
The bounds which Thou hast set,
But oft my unbelief is strong
When floods of woe are met.

Be Thou my steady Anchor, Lord,
Against the tempter's blast;
Speak "Peace be still" to all my fears,
And hold my vessel fast.

Be Thou my Lighthouse in the storm,
And land me safe at last
Upon the blissful shores of peace,
When sorrows all are past.

My Little Burdens

Some of the little hurts
About which I complain,
Would hardly ev'n be noticed
By those who know real pain.

Some of the little weights
Under which now I mourn,
Could hardly be compared with
The burdens some have borne.

None of the little wrongs
Which at my heart have torn,
Should ever ev'n be mentioned
With those my Lord has borne.

O help me, Dearest Lord,
To always be aware,
That any load I carry
With Thine cannot compare.

Help me with patience bear
Whatever falls my lot;
Heav'n will wipe each tear away
And pain will be forgot.

Through Trials We Learn

What checkered paths our feet must trod
If we would truly walk with God;
Our path must wind through valleys dim
If we would learn to trust in Him.

From deep despair a man will cry,
"Dear Lord, have mercy, lest I die."
From views of self a man will flee
To mercy's door on bended knee.

A host of heartaches we must bear
If we would learn to love and care;
Through deep exper'ence we must learn—
A home in heav'n we cannot earn.

A mere profession will not do;
Our walk must prove our faith is true;
Faith must be tried its worth to know
And must be used its pow'r to show.

If we would succor those in pain
We must have felt some of the same;
If we would know what they go through
Their pain we must have suffered too.

If we would learn to empathize
With others when a loved one dies,
We must ourselves lose someone dear
And feel within the grievous tear.

So many things we cannot know
Unless through bitter paths we go;
We learn through trials from day to day
What can't be learned another way.

A Sinner's Prayer
Help us, dear Lord, to trust in Thee
In all our times of woe;
That we may see Thy providence
Unfolding as we go.

O may we ne'er forget our need
Of Thy protecting care,
To keep us from this evil world
And from the devil's snare.

Bless us, dear Lord, from time to time
With Thy sweet presence felt,
And touch us with Thy tender love
Our flinty heart to melt.

O may we ne'er be hardened, Lord
In sin and waywardness;
But when we fall give us the grace
To tearfully confess.

May we not run ahead of Thee
Nor try to walk alone;
For then we'll surely go astray
And reap what we have sown.

May we repose our all in Thee
And lean upon Thy breast;
For 'tis alone in Thee, dear Lord,
That we shall find true rest.

And as we near our final hour
O may we then depart,
With songs of praise upon our lips
And joy within our heart.

⁓⁓⁓

The Seasons of Life

I've seen the beauty of the Spring,
The birds, the buds, the flowers;
I've felt the Summer's torrid heat
And loved its gentle showers.

I've seen the colors of the Fall
And mountains draped with gold
As daylight drew its tendrils in
And night grew crisp and cold

I've felt the Winter's frigid breath
And longed again for Spring,
To see the flowers bloom again
And hear the sparrows sing.

Life, like the seasons, takes its turns
From Spring to Winter's cold;
It is not long from Springtime's youth
'Til we are grey and old.

Just as the seasons swiftly change
The young should realize
How short their journey here will be,
How Spring and Summer flies.

Their Autumn years will soon arrive
And youth will then have flown.
The opportunities of youth
Will be forever gone.

O be not slothful, vile or vain,
While Spring is in full glow;
For thou wilt find thy Wintertime
Is here before you know.

Access in Prayer
At any time of night or day
The child of God may pause and pray.
And though he speak aloud no word
His tho'ts are known, his prayer is heard.

No matter what the courts declare
No law can stop the heart-felt prayer;
Ev'n in a crowded room or hall
The saint upon his God may call.

Into that blessed Holy Place
We have access, thru Christ, by grace;
With silent groans He intercedes
And for us to the Father pleads.

If prayer the Spirit doth indite
The feeblest child can pray aright;
Old Jacob's ladder we may climb
At any place or any time.

Unanswered prayer should not dissuade;
Pray on, dear child, be not dismayed;
God's wisdom far exceeds our own
And what is best by Him is known

Let us not cease to humbly pray;
Our Lord has taught us what to say;
To heaven let us speed our prayer,
The path is clear from here to there.

A Closer Walk with Thee, O God

A closer walk with Thee, O God,
   Should be our highest aim;
Our chief desire in life should be
   To glorify Thy name.

There is no greater pleasure here
   Than in Thy love to dwell,
And feel a holy confidence
   That with our soul 'tis well.

A closer walk with Thee, O God,
   Is worth far more than gold;
It gives us courage in our youth
   And cheers us when we're old.

It saves us from a thousand snares—
   Ten thousand cares and fears;
It helps to hold us on our way,
   And smile through bitter tears.

A closer walk with Thee, O God,
   May we maintain each day!
O may our light shine clear and bright
   Until we pass away!

And ev'n in death may we rejoice
   And from all fear be free,
And give us in that final hour
   A closer walk with Thee!

Just One More Day

Lord, help me thru just one more day,
That may be all I'll need;
May I be guided by Thy word
And oft' upon it feed.

Lord, give me grace for this one day,
Tomorrow is unsure;
E're this day ends my soul may be
In heav'n with Thee secure.

Help me to live today, Dear Lord,
As though it were my last;
I know not what the future holds,
Nor can I change the past.

Let me not fret tomorrow, Lord,
That day may not arrive;
But for today I'll seek Thy face—
For better things I'll strive.

Today is all I'm promised, Lord,
Help me to use it well;
How many days may lie ahead
No mortal man can tell.

Help me to face life's troubles, Lord,
Just one day at a time;
I will not sojourn here for long,
I seek a higher clime.

If Thou should'st give another day
Its needs shall draw my prayer;
And at each turn I am assured
That Thou wilt meet me there.

Lord, bless me now for this one day,
That may be all I'll need;
And if it proves to be my last
I'll then be blest indeed!

Why Art Thou Troubled?

O why, my soul, art thou cast down,
For all things true art thine?
Thy Faith is built on solid ground—
Thy hope on things Divine.

Why should'st thou worry, mope and fret?
Thou hast a faithful God;
His mercy doth sustain thee yet
E'en 'neath His chast'ning rod.

Why art thou troubled, O my soul?
On Him cast all thy care;
Let His felt presence be thy goal
For there's no trouble there.

Who can oppose thee, trembling soul,
If God be on thy side?
'Tis by His grace thou art made whole;
'Twas Christ who bled and died.

My soul, thou needest have no fear
Of endless death and hell,
For through the work of Christ most dear
'Tis with the righteous well.

Hope thou in God, O restless soul,
All trouble soon shall cease
And sheltered safely in His fold
Thou shalt have endless peace!

A Prayer from the Heart

O hallowed Father in the skies,
Majestic, holy, true and wise,
Bless now Thy kingdom thru Thy Son
And may Thy perfect will be done.

May lowly sinners such as we
Oft bow the penitential knee,
And find sweet respite in Thy grace
From conflicts of a fallen race.

Protect us from a dang'rous land
And from the Tempter's treach'rous hand;
We cannot stand in our own pow'r
To triumph in the grievous hour.

Give us, dear Lord, our daily bread
And pour Thy mercies on our head;
May we with truth divine be fed
And daily by Thy hand be led.

Afford us, Lord, a glimpse of Thee
From time to time that we may see
The beauty of Thy holiness,
Our hearts to cheer, our souls to bless.

We thank Thee, Lord, for mercies past
And long to see Thy face at last
In perfect peace with Thee above
To bask in Thy eternal love.

Till death doth waft us from this life
Or Thy return frees us from strife;
With patient hope we'll labor on
With trust in Thee, and Thee alone.

When I Feel My Weakness

2 Corinthians 12:10

When I am weak, then am I strong,
Though many think it strange to say;
But they don't know the paradox
Ev'n though to me it's plain as day.

When I am weak, then am I strong,
For then my weakness I most feel;
To Christ I then more nearly cling,
More often at His throne I kneel.

When I am weak, then am I strong,
For when I'm weak I'm on my knees
Beseeching God to show His face
And do with me as He should please.

When I am weak, then am I strong,
For when I feel my helpless state,
I do not trust in feeble flesh
But on the Lord I humbly wait.

When I am weak, then am I strong,
For then my Lord is all in all;
I look to His great pow'r alone
To keep me lest I slip or fall.

When I am weak, then am I strong,
For in my weakness then I see
That all my strength is in the Lord
And what He does for wretched me.

When I am weak, then am I strong,
And I grow weaker ev'ry day,
But when I bow at heaven's throne
I always stronger come away.

God Has Made a Way

Life will deal its heavy blows
As we meet with bitter foes;
But in spite of all our woes,
God has made a way.

Tho' there seems no way to turn
Through deep sorrows we will learn
And at last we will discern,
God has made a way.

Tho' our path be dark and grim
And our light seems ne'er so dim,
We are still secure in Him,
God has made a way.

Tears may often stain our eyes
But our hoping never dies;
For by grace we realize,
God has made a way.

From the pit of near despair
We will feel His tender care,
And will find each time we're there,
He has made a way.

When we come to face the end
God will timely comfort send,
And with Him we shall ascend,
He has made a way.

Rejoice Ye Blessed Saints

The narrow way that leads to life
Is fraught with fiery trials;
And few the faithful trav'lers there
Who brave the tempter's wiles.
Rejoice! Rejoice! Ye blessed saints
Who walk this hallowed way;
Thy Savior says thy strength shall be
Sufficient for thy day.

Strait is the gate to paths of faith,
Its joys are scarce e'er found;
But to the happy trav'lers there
Sweet peace and love abounds.
Rejoice! Rejoice! ye weary souls,
Though burdened down with sin,
Thy Saviour has declared that faith
The victory shall win.

Strive humbly onward in the way
Thy Savior bids thee go;
In time thy harvest shall be great
As mercies to thee flow.
Rejoice! Rejoice! ye pilgrim friends,
Hold fast the word of grace,
Thy Savior has ascended and
Prepared for thee a place.

O Bless Us, Lord

O Lord, Most High, help us look up
To Thee for all Thy love supplies,
And let us feel in our distress
That Thou dost hear our anguished cries.

O Thou who art the sinner's Hope
And in whose grace we daily trust,
In mercy keep us at Thy feet
Acknowledging that we are dust.

O bless us, Lord, Thy love to feel
When others turn their hearts away;
And give us light within our souls
When outward skies are dark and gray.

O cause Thy face on us to shine
And manifest Thy presence dear,
That we may feel in all our griefs
That Thou dost care and Thou art near.

May we each day from Thee draw strength
And courage to pursue Thy way,
Not fearing what may be the cost
Nor what an evil world may say.

Unworthy though we feel, Dear Lord,
In no one else can we confide
The secrets of our inmost souls
That from Thine eyes we cannot hide.

O Thou in whom we live and move
And have our being and our breath,
Protect us from the tempter's wiles
And kindly cheer us ev'n in death.

I Wish

I wish from time to time to feel
My Savior's presence near,
For this alone restores my soul
And fills my heart with cheer.

I wish to please my Lord and thus
To have His loving smiles;
I long to keep the flesh subdued
And shun the Devil's wiles.

I wish to always humble be
And ne'er with pride to swell;
I long to be where Jesus is
And e'er with Him to dwell.

I wish for meditations pure
With thoughts of things Divine;
I long to walk by faith each day
The old established line.

I wish to be upon my guard
Against the ways of sin,
That while destruction's gate swings wide
I may not enter in.

I wish to walk with saints below
Within fair Zion's gates,
Assured that at the close of time
A better home awaits.

I wish no other hiding place
Than in my Savior's breast;
I long for heaven's matchless sweets
With never-ending rest.

Mercy — The Keynote

In all of our sorrows the Lord is aware
And He will not leave us to utter despair;
His mercy will shine in the darkest of days
And we shall find comfort in its soothing rays.

No trial will grieve us that He has not known,
And where'er we trod He'll not leave us alone;
His presence will cheer us as we press along
And mercy will be the keynote of our song.

The foes we encounter will all be dispersed
And in His great goodness we shall be immersed;
His peace will engulf us when we feel Him near,
And when we are weakest then He is most dear.

O praise Him ye children whose sins are forgiv'n,
His blood has redeemed you and fit you for heav'n;
Give all your devotion to His blessed name,
Proclaim His great goodness and publish His fame.

In life we have found that His promise is sure;
In death we shall find that His grace doth endure;
He'll raise us at last to an unending rest
And in realms of pleasure we'll be ever blest.

Father, I Bow in Thy Presence

Merciful Father, I bow in Thy presence
Knowing Thy power and looking above;
Grant me a sense of Thy manifold mercy,
Bathe my poor heart with sweet tokens of love.

Still Thou my breast with a sense of Thy goodness;
Strip away all that would bar me from Thee;
Grant me a free and sweet unfettered access
As I approach to the great One-in-Three.

Humble me, Lord, with a sense of my vileness
And of the pain Thou hast suffered for me;
Draw me more closely, Lord, into Thy favor
That I may serve Thee and more faithful be.

Help me show kindness to others, Dear Father;
Help me to bridle my tongue all the day;
Help me to show by my life that I love Thee;
Guide me in all that I do or I say.

May my example lead others to praise Thee
And walk in paths of sweet service below,
Finding the joy that exceeds understanding
And the sweet peace that the world cannot know.

Keep Thou my feet, Lord, as onward I struggle;
Let me not falter nor fall by the way;
Take me unto Thee at last, O my Savior,
To that blest haven of unending day.

There I shall praise Thee in robes of perfection,
Joining with millions in songs of delight;
Never to know further pain or dejection
Nor e'er to grope in the darkness of night.

Our Savior Keeps Us

Our Savior keeps us—through all life's dangers,
Through storms and tumults—along the way;
His love is steadfast—to-ward His people
And His compassion—He doth display.

Our Savior keeps us—when we're forsaken
By those we trusted—and thought our friend;
He stays much closer—than any brother
And will be with us—unto the end.

Our Savior keeps us—in times of conflict
When Satan's arrows—upon us fall;
No grief shall conquer—no pain defeat us
For His great mercy—will conquer all.

Our Savior keeps us—when waves of sorrow
Seem to consume us—and sink us low;
His cheering Spirit—is there to lift us
And will deliver—our hearts from woe.

Our Savior keeps us—both night and morning,
When Skies are glowing—and when they're gray;
He's ever faithful—He cannot fail us,
O may we serve Him—love and obey.

Our Savior keeps us—when life is ebbing
And death's chill waters—lie just before,
Then when 'tis finished—O hallelujah!
We shall be with Him—forevermore!

Flee Thou My Soul

Flee thou, my soul, unto the Lord,
Who is thy Chief Delight;
And let no idol gods intrude
To dim or damp thy light.

Flee thou, my soul, unto the Lord
And look to Him for rest;
His yoke is easy, burden light,
His way is good and best.

Flee thou, my soul, unto the Lord
When troubles press thee sore;
His grace sufficient e'er shall be—
Thou canst not ask for more.

Flee thou, my soul, unto the Lord,
On Him cast all thy care;
Why should'st thou struggle with a load
That He hath sworn to bear?

Flee thou, my soul, unto the Lord
While day still sheds its light;
And be not overcome with sin
But cling to truth and right.

Flee thou, my soul, unto the Lord
When tested in the fire;
The test shall not exceed thy strength
But grace will raise thee higher.

Flee thou, my soul, unto the Lord
When death is drawing nigh;
He'll give thee grace to face thy fears
As well as grace to die.

Savior, Help Me

Savior, help me to be humble
As I daily face the foe,
Bearing all the slurs and slanders
That I meet with here below.

Keep me steadfast through the tumult;
Through the struggles keep me strong;
In my conflicts let me conquer
And in sorrow give a song.

As I grapple with life's troubles,
Give me strength to bear the load;
Guide my feet around the pitfalls
Satan places in the road.

Let me not forget to thank Thee
And to praise Thy precious name;
And for all Thy mercies given
Let me noise abroad Thy fame.

When my path seems dark and lonely
Light my feet and show the way;
Give me courage to be faithful,
Help me when I try to pray.

When it seems I can't go farther,
Give me grace to farther go;
How much longer I can labor
Thou alone dost surely know.

When my feeble life is ebbing
And my service here shall cease;
O, then take me, Lord, unto Thee
Where I'll ever live in peace.

I Owe My All to Thee

Thou, Lord, hast given life and breath
And all things good to me;
I am a debtor great indeed—
I owe my all to Thee!

The knowledge of Thy precious word
And truths I'm blest to see
Are worth far more than Ophir's gold;
I owe my all to Thee!

No worthwhile thing hast Thou withheld,
Thy grace is large and free;
And for abundant gifts bestowed
I owe my all to Thee!

A loving wife and children dear
Thou gavest, Lord, to me;
And earthly comforts, not a few—
I owe my all to Thee!

For blessings more than I can count
I humbly bow my knee
To thank Thee from a sincere heart—
I owe my all to Thee!

When lifeless in the grave I lie
My soul in heav'n shall be;
Still owning and confessing thus—
I owe my all to Thee!

Humble Supplications

While we to earth are yet confined,
May we Thy name be praising;
And when we sing may we to *Thee*
Our songs be always raising.

May we be blest, O gracious Lord,
To have Thy sweet approval;
And may our zeal ne'er be disturbed
With languor or removal.

Help us, dear Lord, in our distress
When we are deeply grieving;
When pains of age are pressing hard
And friends from earth are leaving.

Help us in times like these to feel
A blessed consolation;
That all our faith and hope is built
Upon a firm foundation.

May Thy pure words be our delight,
Our only rule for living;
And of the good we are supplied
Be always freely giving.

May we complete our race with joy,
And on that glad tomorrow,
Take us to Thee on wings of love
Away from sin and sorrow.

More Faithful to Be

The closer we live to our Savior above,
The more we will bask in His tokens of love.

The more we approach the rich throne of His grace,
The more we will feel His delightful embrace.

The more time we spend in His glorious word,
The more will our prayers be acceptably heard.

The more we conform to His will and His ways,
The shorter our nights and the sweeter our days.

The more of His truth we absorb and digest,
The stronger we grow and the more we are blest.

The more we depend on His mercy and grace,
The better prepared our afflictions to face.

The more we are tried and the greater our load,
The more will His mercy on us be bestowed.

The more we reflect on His mercy and love,
The brighter our hope of the glory above.

The more we partake in His sufferings and death,
The less we will dread our approaching last breath.

O bless us, Dear Lord, to live closer to Thee,
More grace to enjoy and more faithful to be.

God's Little Ones

Thy little ones, O gracious Lord,
Are special in Thy sight;
Who know and feel their wretchedness
And look to Thee for light.

They know their utter helplessness
Without Thy strength Divine;
And like a tender little babe,
Their all to Thee resign.

Like little children they depend
Upon Thy faithful care;
They trust that in their ev'ry need
Thou shalt be always there.

They look to Thee for daily bread
And give their thanks anew,
For ev'ry favor Thou dost give
And blessings not a few.

They love to feel Thy presence near,
It makes them feel secure;
They love Thy truth because they know
Its ev'ry line is sure.

They cannot hope for heav'n above
Apart from Thy rich grace,
Nor can they trust in flesh and blood
To help them in their race.

They love Thy promise, pure and true,
Of rest beyond this vale;
And have a child-like confidence,
Thy promise cannot fail.

Consolation in our Troubles

Through the darkness and the danger
God has kept us by His grace;
Through the deadness and the dying
He has shown His loving face.

In the midst of tribulation,
Through the tumults and the tears,
He has given consolation
And allayed our doubts and fears.

Through the painful persecutions
We have felt His presence dear;
He has given perseverance
When we feared the end was near.

Through our faintings and our failings
He has faithfully secured,
All our feeble, falt'ring footsteps
And by grace we have endured.

He has never failed to bless us
In the darkest of our trials;
And when frowns of earth were greatest,
We have felt His loving smiles.

He has taught us thus to trust Him
Even in our bleakest hours;
For no matter how we've suffered
He has strewn our path with flowers.

And the beauty that awaits us
Over on the other shore,
Will make up for all our sufferings;
O! for grace to love Him more!

Under God's Care

When low in the valley, our Savior is there
A faithful Companion, our troubles to bear;
In seasons of tempest, foul weather or fair,
His mercy encircles—we're under His care.

In times of thick darkness, He still guides our feet,
In springtime and harvest, thru cold and thru heat;
He will not forsake us nor withdraw His hand,
Our life and its changes are at His command.

Thru sickness and sorrow He knows all our needs
And as our Physician, He nurtures and feeds;
His healing is pleasant, a balm for the soul,
He speaks words of comfort and hearts are made whole.

When friends are unfaithful and Satan is near,
He proves His affection—our prayers He will hear;
His promise is certain for He cannot lie,
Nor shall He e'er leave us for He cannot die.

He keeps all His children secure in His love,
And grace has assured them a place far above;
He always protects them—His love cannot fail,
And thus by His mercy they all shall prevail.

He will not relinquish one soul to the foe,
For whom He has borne all their mis'ry and woe;
Because He has suffered and paid for their sin,
They cannot be charged with the same debt again.

He'll ever be with us, ev'n to our last breath;
He keeps us in life and upholds us in death;
Then sorrow is ended and joy reigns supreme
Where saints join in praising their Savior and King.

In the Valley Distressed[5]

Great God, when we feel in the valley distressed
And hardly can rise 'neath the load;
Then wilt Thou descend in Thy mercy to bless
And hear from Thy blessed abode?

When darkness descends and envelops our souls,
Send light and illumine our way;
That we may again feel to be in Thy fold,
And thus give us strength as our day.

O let us not languish and grieve or repine
But lift us above all our foes;
Deliver our souls from the tempter's design
And keep us from all grievous woes.

O give grace to bear all the sorrows and tears
That come to us here while below;
And help us to bear all the world's scornful sneers
That we may Thy love sweetly show.

And when Thou art finished with us here in time,
May we have a sweet hour to die;
And on that great morn when the dead shall arise,
Take us home with Thee to the sky.

✺

May I Never Forget

May I ne'er forget the favors
That on me the Lord has shed,
Ever mindful that He leads me
And that daily I am fed.

---

[5] The words to this poetry may be sung to the tunes of any of the following hymns: *Adoration* (No. 33), *Lone Pilgrim* (No. 150), or *O Thou in Whose Presence* (No. 420) in *Old School Hymnal, Eleventh Edition.*

May I ne'er forget the mercy
That so freely He bestowed,
When within my heart so gently
He established His abode.

May I ne'er forget the feeling
When I saw my sins forgiv'n,
And was blest to view Christ dying
That my home might be in heav'n.

May I ne'er forget His suff'rings—
Far too great for us to know;
And the vast and wondrous mercies
That from these great suff'rings flow.

May I ne'er forget the chast'nings
Which have kept me near His feet,
Nor the merciful restorings
So abasing, yet so sweet!

May I ne'er forget the moments
When I've felt His presence near,
When I've sensed His sweet approval
And His loving smile so dear.

May I ne'er forget petitions
That from bleeding heart were made;
And the kind, amazing answers
He has graciously displayed.

Thank you, Lord, for all Thy blessings
To a sinner weak and lame;
May I ne'er forget Thy goodness
But forever praise Thy name.

God's Faithful Care

When gloom draws near and clouds are low,
May we not fear a flood of woe;
Our Lord has promised to sustain
And to be with us through our pain.

Let us not languish when all seems lost;
He knows our anguish when we're tossed
By vicious waves of doubt and fear,
And He has promised e'er to be near.

No ill shall rise that He cannot cure;
Our comfort lies in His promise sure;
He will be faithful to His word
And blessings sweet shall be conferred.

We are secure in His loving hand;
We shall endure and finally stand
Glorified in His righteousness,
Eternally His name to bless.

May we find peace in what He has done
And never cease to praise His Son,
For His redeeming love and grace
Shown by preparing us a place.

When we draw near the gates of death,
May we not fear the last struggling breath;
He will give grace in that final hour
And take us sweetly to His bower.

Looking Unto Jesus

There is much on earth to tempt us
And to lead our steps astray;
Let us keep our eyes on Jesus,
Let us hold upon our way.

When the waves of trouble pound us
And we're threatened by the gale,
Let us keep our eyes on Jesus
And by grace we shall prevail.

Doubts and fears will oft assail us
As we live from day to day;
Let us keep our eyes on Jesus;
He will drive those fears away.

Satan hopes he will defeat us
And at times he may succeed;
Let us keep our eyes on Jesus,
He will give the strength we need.

There are times when trouble lays us
Low and strives to keep us there;
Let us keep our eyes on Jesus,
He will all our troubles share.

By and by when death approaches
And our nat'ral sight is weak,
May we keep our eyes on Jesus;
He will give the grace we seek.

Then when we awake in heaven,
Ne'er again to be afraid,
We will keep our eyes on Jesus
And the sight will never fade.

Jesus Hears and Answers Prayer

When the way is dark and drear
And our hearts are filled with fear,
    Jesus knows our ev'ry care;
He will hear and answer prayer.

He will hear and answer prayer,
    Seated with our Father there,
    Interceding with all care;
Jesus hears and answers prayer.

Though my groanings silent be,
    Jesus hears my feeble plea;
    In my closet He is there,
Knows my heart and hears my prayer.

Jesus hears and answers prayer,
    Though I wonder here and there;
Stam'ring though my prayers may be
    Jesus intercedes for me.

Daniel in the Lion's den,
    Shut away from earthly friend,
    Yet the Lord was with him there;
Jesus heard and answered prayer.

Jesus heard and answered prayer,
    Saved His servant from the snare;
Brought him through with not a tear;
    Jesus heard and answered prayer.

Jesus, O Thou faithful friend,
First great Cause and last great End;
    E're we bow before Thy throne
All our needs and cares are known.

Thou wilt hear and answer prayer,
Thy great love with us to share;
Thou wilt free us from all care;
Thou dost hear and answer prayer.

A Blest People[6]

How blest are those who know the Lord
And find sweet comfort in His word!
And though their path grows sometimes dim,
Yet still their trust resides in Him
And He their joy shall be.

He is their God, their life, their all,
Before Whom they with reverence fall;
And on Him oft they humbly call,
And plead for His amazing grace
To guide them on their way.

In Him their faith and hope abides,
And oft in Him their soul confides;
Their hope of heav'n in Him resides,
And they, when life on earth is o'er
With Him shall ever be.

---

[6] This poem may be sung to the tune of "O Love That Will Not Let Me Go" No. 507 in *Old School Hymnal, Eleventh Edition.*

When Discouraged

When sore beset with grievous woes
And all within us seems to groan,
We need to turn our eyes toward heav'n
And realize we're not alone.

Our Lord knows every pain we feel,
For He endured far worse than we;
His suff'rings far exceeded ours
And *His* were caused by you and me.

Consider all the pleasant days
When trouble did not press us sore;
And then take comfort in the thought
That there are blessings yet in store.

God's mercies do not reach a point
Where they abruptly cease to flow;
But better days lie out ahead
And sweeter times we soon shall know.

God could have cast us *all* away
And yet remained a righteous King;
And when we rightly mull this truth,
It gives us cause His praise to sing.

Things could be worse, far more severe,
If we our just deserts received;
We could have been among the lost
Whose miseries ne'er shall be relieved.

May we in all infirmities
Like Paul, now glory in their sting;
And know that in God's loving hands
They are a truly blessed thing.

There is no need to be cast down
For soon the clouds will disappear;
The Lord will give us fresh resolve
And to His bosom draw us near.

❦

When the Lord is Near
When feelingly the Lord is near,
How sweet a season it affords!
How joyous is a visit from
The King of kings and Lord of lords!

It makes all sorrows flee away,
While sweetly we with Him commune;
And then we find to our dismay,
Such seasons pass away too soon!

We long to have Him come again
And bathe us with His quick'ning breath;
And with our inner man renewed
To have no fear of life or death.

There are no words for times like these;
Our feelings cannot be expressed,
While in His love we sweetly bask,
And lay our heads upon His breast.

How precious 'tis to feel that love
Around us whether day or night;
And feel a fresh resolve within
That we shall ne'er give up the fight!

Such seasons make our spirits soar
Beyond these lowly, temp'ral scenes;
Hence we learn more what heav'n is
And what true pleasure really means.

Oh give us more such seasons, Lord,
That more like Thee our souls may be;
And keep us in Thy love until
We safely dwell in heav'n with Thee.

Precious Faith

By faith the patriarchs of old
O'ercame the powers of hell;
Before their faith no foe could stand
And walls of cities fell.

By faith dear Abraham went forth,
Not knowing where he went;
But confident beyond all doubt,
That he by heav'n was sent.

By faith brave Moses turned his back
Upon dark Egypt's gold;
And chose instead to bear reproach
With God's afflicted fold.

By faith great kingdoms were subdued,
And mouths of lion's stopped;
Great armies turned and fled away
And all their weapons dropped.

And on and on the list might go
Of faith's amazing deeds;
And now, by faith, we likewise walk
And go where Jesus leads.

By faith we know the worlds were framed
By His almighty hand;
And all our troublers must retreat
At His divine command.

O, help us, Lord, to humbly trust,
And put our faith in Thee;
And look to Thee for present help
And final victory.

⌘

Manifold Mercies
Thou hast blest me from conception,
God of mercy and of truth;
Thou hast spared me in my weakness
And the foolishness of youth.

Early didst Thou show Thy favor
And reveal to me my sin;
Made me trust in Christ completely
To remove the guilt within.

Thou didst bring me to Thy table
Where a feast had been prepared;
And I oft with saints have gathered
And those heav'nly cordials shared.

Thou didst place within a burden
To declare Thy wondrous grace;
And I've acted on that burden,
Where there was for me a place.

Thou hast given me a family
And a host of precious friends,
To stand with me in life's battles,
Till my earthly journey ends.

Thou hast placed a hope of heaven
Deep within my longing heart;

And from that sweet hope of Glory,
I wish never to depart.

Thou hast promised to stand by me
Ne'er to leave me nor forsake;
Hence I look for life eternal,
When in Glory I awake.

Thoughts of a Sinner[7]
How oft does my heart seem to stray
Away from the things of the Lord;
And seek to find comfort in earth's fickle toys
Instead of the truths of His word!

This body of flesh pulls me down
And hinders my walk with the Lord;
It grieves me to think of the joys I have lost
When His wondrous truth I've ignored.

What sorrow to think of the days
I've wasted in worthless pursuits;
And failed to appeal to the word of the Lord
And savor its heavenly fruits!

O, how can the Lord condescend
To one so unworthy as me?
O, how can He show such compassion and love,
And bless me His wonders to see?

'Tis by His rich grace, if at all,
That heaven's bright realms I shall see;
And not by the deeds of my poor feeble flesh,
Praise be! His salvation is free!

---

[7] This poem may be sung to the tune of "When Sorrows Encompass Me Round," No. 339 in *The Good Old Songs.*

O, join me in praising His name!
How good and how great is His love!
How sweet is the hope that we soon shall behold,
That wonderful home up above!

***

A View of Christ on the Cross
Adoring, I gaze on my Lord
By faith, as He hangs on the tree;
And marvel that blood so submissively shed
Could cover a wretch such as me.

I see as I look on His face
A tear and a smile blend as one;
And wonder as I stand in awe of the scene,
Could He include me as a son?

I fall 'neath the cross on my knees
With tears running down from my face;
And cry, "Are my sins charged to Him as He bleeds,
And does He now die in my place?"

A glimpse from His agonized face
Assures me of covenant grace;
And love beyond words floods my penitent heart,
As I look again on His face.

Such beauty I cannot express,
As this morbid scene now unfolds;
And I contemplate the great price that He paid
For millions of sanctified souls.

And though my heart bleeds for His pain,
Yet lift I my face to the skies;
Words fail me to pen this unspeakable scene,
As He so triumphantly dies.

Oh, do I mistake His design,
And have I been wrong in it all?
Then why this deep love that burns hot in my breast,
And why do I yet on Him call?

I'll hope in His mercy till death,
And ne'er begrudge one temp'ral loss;
But cling to the glory I felt when I viewed
My Lord as He hung on the cross.

～～∞～～

Pilgrim, Are You Troubled?
Pilgrim, are you troubled
By your guilt and sin?
Do you feel forsaken
And without a friend?

Don't despair, my kinsman,
We are sinners too;
We can witness with those
Pains you're passing through.

Turn your eyes t'ward Jesus;
He has suffered too;
And can empathize with
Weary souls like you.

Children, are you fearful
Of the road ahead?
Does it fill your heart with
Pangs of doubt and dread?

Don't despair, dear servants,
We have felt your fear:
We have known your faintings,
Unbelief was near.

Look upon our Savior;
He has conquered fear;
His delightful presence
Fills our hearts with cheer.

Soldiers are you weary
Of the raging fight?
Have you thought of turning
From this weary plight?

Don't despair, dear comrades,
Though we faltered too,
Jesus has sustained us,
He has seen us through.

Wear the Christian armor;
Victory is sure;
Jesus is our Captain
And we shall endure.

A Never-Ending Song

As we plod along, burdens ever strong,
Jesus is our constant stay;
Gives us grace to live, labor, love and give,
And to hold upon our way.

His sustaining love helps us rise above
All the trials we must bear;
And His promise sweet is a sure retreat,
For we know that He doth care.

We are weak and frail and we often fail,
But we have a faithful friend;
He will safely guide through the swelling tide,
And will keep us to the end.

He can never fail and He must prevail
O'er the forces of the world;
And his providence is a sure defense
When the darts of sin are hurled.

In the final day when we fly away
In the likeness of our Lord;
The redemption song will be pure and strong,
And we'll sing in sweet accord.

Heaven will resound with the joyful sound
Of the great elected throng;
As their praise abounds to the Great "I AM"
In a never ending song.

***

I Thank Thee, Lord
I thank Thee, Lord, for Thy rich grace
That gave me life divine,
And showed me that all glory for
This precious gift is thine.

I thank Thee for that inward work
That made me see my sin,
And know that in my flesh alone
No good abides therein.

I thank Thee for Thy guiding hand
That brought me to Thy feet,
And made me know my only hope
Was at Thy mercy seat.

I thank Thee, Lord, for ev'ry tear
That brought me nearer Thee;
I thank Thee for each grievous pain
That drove me to my knees.

I thank Thee for the chastening rod
That oft' has made me weep,
That I might learn Thy statutes well
And all Thy precepts keep.

I Thank Thee for all timely joys
And heav'nly blessings too,
And for the knowledge that Thy word
Is pure and good and true.

For things too numerous to express
Accept my thanks and praise;
And may I to Thy precious name
Eternal anthems raise.

⁕

A Contrite Heart—A Secret Key
A broken and a contrite heart,
The Lord will not despise;
And those who have this humble trait
Are precious in His eyes.
    —Psalm 51:17

The sacrifices of this heart,
Burnt off'rings far exceeds;
And in these God doth take delight
As worthy, righteous deeds.

A spirit humble and contrite,
The Lord doth oft' revive;
And to achieve this blessed state
The saints should daily strive.
    —Isaiah 57:15

Yea, to those saints the Lord will look
Who tremble at His word,
Who feel and know their poverty,
And walk in sweet accord.
—Psalm 66.2

A secret key do those possess
Who have a contrite heart;
And all who own this humble frame,
In heaven have a part.

The Key to Many Blessings
Let us lay aside all brashness,
And all vanity and pride;
Let us be as little children,
With the humble to reside.

Never haughty or highminded;
Never full of self or vain;
But abiding with the lowly,
Counting all our loss as gain.

Christ, Himself, was meek and lowly,
And we ought to be like Him;
All His attributes are lovely;
Let us always treasure them.

There are none who shine so brightly
As the little lambs of God;
Those who've known divine correction,
And have passed beneath the rod.

They are contrite and submissive
To the perfect will of God;
For their hearts have been made tender
And with meekness have been shod.

'Tis to these God looks with favor;
'Tis to these the Lord is nigh;
He is with them in their troubles;
He is with them when they die.

Let us strive to be more humble;
'Tis a precious Christian grace;
'Tis the key to many blessings;
Let us meekly fill our place.

Hated by Men but Loved by God

My faith in the Lord keeps me striving,
Midst evils like mountains around;
I know that His pow'r has sustained me,
In spite of the world's wicked frown.

I often sink low in the valley,
But not to the point of despair;
I feel that God's love is there with me,
And keeps me from Satan's dread snare.

Great lairs have been oft laid to ruin me,
But out of them all I've been freed;
By God's gracious workings of mercy,
He kindly has met every need.

In striving to walk in His precepts,
I've often had darts thrown my way;
But all of those darts were deflected,
By Him to whom daily I pray.

He told us that we would be hated,
Because we are not of this world;
But then when we're saddest and lowest,
His banner of love is unfurled.

There's coming a day, and we know it,
When He shall descend with a shout;
And all of the saints will fly upward
To realms where there'll be no more doubt.

I'm looking with anticipation
To that great deliverance day;
Where never again we'll know sorrow,
And nothing can darken our way.

Never Give Up

Way-worn pilgrim ne'er give up,
Though you drink the bitter cup;
Soon with Christ thy soul will sup
    —Always faithful be.
'Tis a fleeting journey here,
Death is ever drawing near;
But we ought not faint or fear
    —Bliss we soon shall see!

Ev'n in darkest shades of night,
Let us ne'er give up the fight;
Striving e'er for truth and right
    —God will give us grace!
Ours is not a life of ease
As we strive our Lord to please;
But by living on our knees
    —We will win the race!

O thou servants of our God,
Though discouraged onward trod;
Soon we'll leave this earthly sod
    —And find rest above!

What a joyous time t'will be,
Fully clothed with victory,
Basking for eternity
—In our Savior's love!

❧

A Contrite Heart

A contrite heart—a wondrous gift!
It keeps its owners on their knees;
To God its kind petitions lift
And seeks alone His will to please.

A contrite heart—it will not vaunt
Itself, or seek a higher seat;
Its gifts it will not seek to flaunt,
But strives to live at Jesus' feet.

A contrite heart—it will esteem
Its brother better than itself;
To evil words and worldly themes
It ever seeketh to be deaf.

A contrite heart—it only seeks
To live in humble, sweet accord;
To speak in gentle accents meek,
And want no other than its Lord.

A contrite heart—it seeks to do
To others as it would be done;
It wishes to be ever true
And strives the Christian race to run.

A contrite heart—it often kneels,
And yields entirely to God's will;
The grief of others oft' it feels,
And sympathizes with their ills.

A contrite heart—it humbly waits
For heaven's joys—eternal—sweet;
And when within those calming gates,
Its hopes will then be all complete.

The Storms of Life

The storms they come, they rage, they blow,
And God alone their course doth know,
But by His word we understand
All powers must yield to His command.

The elements bow to His will
When His command is, "Peace, be still."
He rides upon the fiercest storm
And triumphs in most glorious form.

And just as He can still the wind,
So He can give sweet peace within;
The weakest heart He can address
And give it calm repose and rest.

There is no inner storm so great
That His great power cannot abate;
His soothing touch can calm the soul
And make the weakest trembler bold.

All things are in His mighty hand;
He rules and reigns on sea and land;
In all things we should thus concede
What pleases Him is what we need.

"What is His will?" should be our quest,
Assured His way is always best;
No other way can e'en compare,
For it is perfect, pure and fair.

Then when the storms of life are near,
May He assist us not to fear;
But with our all on Him rely,
Assured that He is always nigh.

We Shall at Last Prevail

How faulty are our efforts
To run the Christian race!
And we would fail completely
If not for God's rich grace.

Our sinful flesh would ruin us
If grace did not prevent;
And we would sink forever
If mercies were not sent.

The world doth oft distress us
And every cov'nant break;
But Christ will never leave us
Nor will He e'er forsake.

The devil and his angels
Seek only to devour;
But Jesus keeps us safely,
Because He has all power.

Life's daily trials and burdens
Oft seem too great to bear;
But then we learn how greatly
The Lord for us doth care.

Our steps are often hindered
In ways we don't expect;
But God has promised ever
To love us and protect.

In spite of all against us,
We shall at last prevail;
For God Himself is for us,
And He can never fail.

O, What a Gracious God!

How precious are Thy mercies, Lord,
To poor unworthy souls like me;
And what a gracious God Thou art
To grant that we may worship Thee!

How privileged we are, Dear Lord,
To be raised out of bondage sore;
To live with heart fixed on the skies
And thus to serve the flesh no more!

How deep were we immersed in sin,
And thought there was true pleasure there;
Until Thy Spirit shined within
And freed us from the devil's lair!

We had remained in sin's embrace
If Thou hadst not reached down Thy hand;
And on a Rock our feet did place,
And lead us to Thy Canaan's Land.

What words could ever tell the whole
Of mercy so extremely great;
Or of the gift of life divine
Entitling to a vast estate?

At last we'll fully realize
The beauty and the glory of
The precious treasures Thou hast giv'n,
And all the wonders of Thy love.

For all eternity Thy saints
Shall sing of Thy amazing grace,
Delighting in the joys of Heav'n
And basking in Thy sweet embrace.

≈≈

I Only Wish a Lowly Place
I do not seek the world's esteem
Nor long for it's reward;
I only wish a lowly place
In union with my Lord.

I do not yearn for wealth or fame
Nor seats of power and might;
I only seek a humble walk
With Christ in truth and light.

Give me the lowest place, Dear Lord,
Just so I have Thy smiles;
And always walk close by my side
In comforts *and* in trials.

Keep me aware that I am dust
And always stand in need
Of Thy sustaining grace and love,
My cause in Heaven to plead.

The least of saints I feel to be
If I am one at all;
The chief of sinners I must be
And ruined by the Fall.

But Thou hast given precious hope
In Thy redeeming grace;
And tho' my flesh is black as death
I long to see Thy face.

I'll go on hoping till the end
That in the final hour,
I'll be raised up to endless praise
By Thy almighty power.

⁓⁓⁓

A Beggar I Am
I am a beggar, poor and weak
And lay at mercy's door;
And even when the door seems shut,
God's grace I yet implore.
For there is no place else to go—
There is no other source;
His promises can never fail,
His word He doth enforce.

A beggar such as I must bow
At Jesus' blessed feet;
And plead his cause with spirit meek
Before the mercy seat.
He has no merit he can plead
But comes with empty hand,
And casts his all upon the Lord
And begs for grace to stand.

A beggar cannot vaunt himself
Nor dictate what he's given;
He thus receives with heart-felt thanks
Gratuities of heaven.
He knows that any alms he's given
Are more than he deserves;
And thus with gratitude he lives
And lovingly he serves.

A beggar I will ever be
Until the Lord's return;
And then I hope for heaven's bliss
A place I did not earn.
If I'm an heir of God's rich grace
Then royalty is mine;
And I will bask eternally
In riches all divine.

Unworthy Am I

Unworthy, unworthy, unworthy am I,
To have the least blessing, or have Christ draw nigh;
Not one crumb of merit doth my flesh possess;
I'm naught but a beggar, my soul must confess.

If I am an heir of the regions above,
It must be by mercy and infinite love;
If there is within me the least bit of worth,
It all comes through Jesus, and heavenly birth.

I did not determine whose child I would be
For that was God's option in eternity;
If I am His child it is all of His grace,
I ne'er would have otherwise seen His sweet face.

While dead in my sins I could not make the choice;
It took pow'r divine in His quickening voice;
I could not desire what my flesh did refuse
Nor could I despise what my nature did choose.

No credit I claim for the Spirit within
'Twas purely a gift from my Heavenly Friend;
I ne'er would have served Him if left on my own;
Bad seed are the only ones I would have sown.

I know it was mercy, and mercy alone,
That caused Christ to die and my sins to atone;
I hope I may serve Him from now till I die
And then rise to meet Him and praise Him on high.

My debt is so great I could never repay
But I shall keep striving till I'm swept away,
To realms pure and blissful where I shall e'er sing,
"My worthiness lies in my Savior and King."

Ponderings of a Poor Sinner

Oh! Can it be, most gracious Lord,
That *I*, so vile, am truly thine?
It seems too much—too great for words—
That such a joy is really *mine!*

Shall such a worthless wretch as *I*
Traverse the realms of bliss on high?
Shall *I* see Jesus by and by
And in His blessed bosom lie?

Why am *I* blessed to love the Lord
When hoards of others never do?
Why do *I* treasure all His word
While throngs deny that He is true?

Why did the Lord reach down His hand
And lift *me* from the sinking sand,
While millions sink down to despair
And seem content to languish there?

Such thoughts are far too high for me;
Oh, how can such great wonders be?
Yet in this hope I live each day
That Christ has put my sins away.

Such things are often on my mind
And answers oft I never find;
But though I have so little light,
I know that all God does is right.

One day these things will all be clear;
Our queries all will disappear;
Then we shall know as we are known
And doubts and fears will all be gone.

⸻

Cast Thy Burden on the Lord[8]
Cast thy burden on the Lord,
Only lean upon His Word;
Thou wilt soon have cause to bless
His eternal faithfulness.

He sustains thee by His hand,
He enables thee to stand;
Those whom Jesus once hath loved
From His grace are never moved.

Human counsels come to naught,
That shall stand which God hath wrought;
His compassion, love, and power,
Are the same forevermore.

Heav'n and earth may pass away,
God's free grace shall not decay;
He hath promised to fulfill
All the pleasure of His will.

---

[8] Verses 1-5 by Roland Hill, 1783; Verses 6-7 by Elder Ralph Harris, June 7, 2005.

Jesus, Guardian of Thy flock,
Be Thyself our constant Rock;
Make us, by Thy powerful hand,
Strong as Zion's mountain stand.

Thou art our eternal rest,
Favored we, and greatly blest;
Anchored to the courts above
By Thy never-ending love.

When we come, O Lord, to die,
Let our souls to Thee draw nigh;
Peacefully to take their flight
Into Thy eternal light.

"Faint, Yet Pursuing" — Judges 8:4

I often am grieved by the world's vain alluring
And groan 'neath the weight of my own unwise doing;
But I'm still pressing onward, — "faint, yet pursuing."

I fear lest my sins should become my undoing
And could not go on but for God's kind renewing;
Thus I still struggle onward, — "faint, yet pursuing."

Lord, help me to vanquish all evils ensuing;
Be always close by, and my foes be subduing;
Thou knowest that I am still — "faint, yet pursuing."

In life's daily conflicts my faults I'm oft ruing,
But thoughts of Thy mercy I'm ever reviewing;
On my knees I remain, Lord, — "faint, yet pursuing."

Lord, I long every day for Thy gracious bedewing
When faith ends in sight and sweet heaven I'm viewing;
Then I'll never again be — "faint, yet pursuing."

How Blest are the Sheep!

How blest are the sheep of the Dear Master's fold
Who rest by the still water's side,
And feast on the manna He gives young and old
As near Him they humbly reside!

How peaceful the place where His presence is felt
And love is so feelingly near;
Where souls at His feet are repentantly knelt
And there is no dimness or fear!

How sweet are the hours when their flesh is subdued
And love draws them near to His breast;
When sorrows are vanquished and faith is renewed
And they with assurance are blest!

How sad, then, the times when the Lord seems withdrawn
And they seem to seek Him in vain;
But He will in time make His rich intent known
And all of His purposes plain!

How kind are His mercies to unworthy souls
Who have naught of merit to claim!
How good that He rules, that He reigns, and controls
And lifts up the poor and the lame!

How feeble the saints, yet by His wondrous power,
He keeps them and sets them apart;
He ne'er will desert them—not even an hour—
But treasures them near to His heart!

How great is the joy that for them doth await
At last when this journey is o'er;
As they 'round the throne of the Lord congregate
And, there, praise His name ever more!

In His Presence

In God's presence there is glory
And there's majesty untold;
And one touch of His sweet Spirit
Is worth more than Ophir's gold.

In His presence there is sweetness
Such as never can be told;
It can calm the fretting infant
And can cheer both young and old.

In His presence cares will vanish
And sweet promises unfold;
Hearts will soar on wings like eagles
And the timid may wax bold.

In His presence there is wonder
And great beauty to behold;
There is awe, and there is splendor,
And the half has ne'er been told.

In His presence there's renewing
For the hearts that have grown cold;
And from hung'ring, thirsting children,
No good thing will He withhold.

In His presence bow with rev'rence
As the sheep of His great fold;
Come with tender hearts submissive
And with burdens on Him rolled.

In His presence saints will shelter
When at last the story's told;
And their joys will be eternal
In that land where none grows old.

An Uneven Pathway

The life of God's people is varied,
Sometimes they will feel so alone;
Much weeping oft comes in the darkness,
But joy doth appear at the dawn.

It would not be best if they always
Were high on the mountains of joy;
There must be some conflicts to try them,
Their dross to root out and destroy.

Say, how could they e'er be exalted
If always they dwelt in the clouds?
Without the sore school of affliction,
They always would go with the crowds.

They must be brought down in the valley
Before they can leap on the hills;
They must pass through seasons of suff'ring
Before they can know heaven's thrills.

If not for the deep, threat'ning shadows,
How could they know darkness from light?
If not for their own wretched weakness,
How could they know God's pow'r and might?

God's wisdom is seen in His dealings
With His little children so dear;
He first makes them feel their unfitness
Before they're drawn feelingly near.

At last He will take them to Glory
Where they will forever be blest;
Where all of their conflicts are over
And they are forever at rest.

At this Moment

At this moment God is reigning up in heaven,
And is ruling in the power of His might;
He, immortal, sits in splendor in yon haven
Clothed with glory far exceeding earthly light.

Yet He condescends to dwell among we mortals
Ev'n to live within the hearts of His dear sheep,
And is working out His purpose ev'ry moment
Ever mindful of His promises to keep.

At this moment He is thinking of His people
And with care He is providing for their needs;
He protects and guards and shields His own from danger
And His hungering lambs He daily tends and feeds.

At this moment He is mindful of their sorrows
And aware of ev'ry conflict that they feel;
He will mend the wounds that oft have been inflicted
And the broken hearted He will kindly heal.

At this moment His compassion toward them hastens
And He's filling aching hearts with His great love;
He is giving them assurance of His favor
And is showering them with blessings from above.

At this moment He's aware of ev'ry heartbeat,
Ev'ry motion, ev'ry movement, in the world;
And at last His glorious purpose will be clearer
As His word is all fulfilled and truth unfurled.

At this moment we who love Him are awaiting
That sweet moment when in glory He appears;
Taking all His children with Him up to heaven
Where there are no further sorrows, pains or tears.

The Promises of God

God's sweet promises, so blessed,
O how precious to the saints!
What a bulwark they afford us,
And they leave no place for chance!

O those blessed words of comfort
That descend from heav'n above;
So delightful in their essence,
And a token of His love!

O that wonderful salvation
By His promise made secure!
Were it not for this assurance
Not a blessing would be sure.

He has promised ne'er to leave us
And has sworn He'll ne'er forsake;
Could there be a greater promise?
Let us from it comfort take.

He has promised grace sufficient,
Ev'ry burden to endure.
O how sweet to think upon it!
O how pleasant, and how pure!

Let us lean upon His promise
As we live from day to day;
Let us put aside our doubting
As we seek the narrow way.

He who cannot lie has promised,
And by grace we do believe,
He will comfort us when dying
And our soul He will receive.

Who Else?

To whom besides Thee shall we go,
O gracious Lord most high?
Alone in Thee is life divine
And none with Thee can vie.

Where else can sinners such as we
Find lasting peace and rest?
No other comfort can be found
In whom we may be blest.

To whom else can we make our prayers
And hope to gain an ear?
And who but Thee has said that he
The prayer of faith will hear?

Who else but Thee can see within
Our aching, bleeding heart?
And make us feel that tho' we're vile,
In Thee we have a part?

Who else but Thee can soothe our fears
And calm our anxious breast?
Who else can give us fresh resolve
To try to do our best?

Who else but Thee could take our sin
And put it all away,
So that it ne'er could be recalled
At any future day?

Who else can raise us when we fall
And bless us ev'n in death?
Who else can fill our failing hearts
With joy in our last breath?

O, How Vital are Thy Blessings![9]

O, how vital are Thy blessings
Lord of life and God of peace!
Thus we come to Thee confessing
Without Thee our joy would cease.

In the midst of tribulation,
May we ever look to Thee,
For the grace to keep our station
And to ever humble be.

When it seems our foes compass us
And the darkness closes in;
Let not unbelief harass us
But revive our hope again.

Let us view Thee in Thy beauty
And rise up as though on wings,
Strengthened in our faith and duty
And with thoughts of higher things.

May our hearts be firm and stable
As we face the days ahead;
Ever mindful Thou art able
To supply our daily bread.

Thus when life is from us leaving
And our souls to Thee ascend,
Let there be no bitter grieving
But a song of peace within.

---

[9] These words may be sung to the tune "Love Divine," No. 60 in *Old School Hymnal, Eleventh Edition.*

In My Distress
In my distress, to God I've cried,
And He has heard my plea;
No better place I've found when tried
Than on the bended knee.

In my distress I've hoped for grace
To get me through the trial;
And when He's shown His smiling face,
I've rested for awhile.

In my distress, I thank Thee Lord,
That Thou hast giv'n relief;
And turning to Thy blessed word
Has helped me in my grief.

In my distress may I recall
Thine own exceeding pain;
Compared to Thine, my pains are small,
Their mention seemeth vain.

In my distress, Lord, let me run
To Thee and find reprieve;
Until at last my race is done
And Thou my woes relieve.

In my distress I'll struggle on
Relying on Thy grace;
And finally that day will dawn
Where trouble has no place.

No more distress! O, can it be,
That such will be my lot?
To have a place of endless glee
Where grief is all forgot.

Wait, Humbly Wait

Almighty King, admired by those
Who know their wretched state;
May we on Thee alone depend,
Upon Thee let us wait.

Upon Thee let us wait, Dear Lord,
And cast our all on Thee;
And may Thy loving providence
Our constant shelter be.

Whene'er our path is strewn with doubt
And hope is growing dim,
Let us not fail to flee to Christ
And humbly wait on Him.

Wait on His wise and timely aid—
He always knows what's best;
With patience do what He commands,
And leave to Him the rest.

Wait, humbly wait, and seek His will,
Strive not to race ahead;
If we go trusting in His word,
By Him we shall be led.

Where Would I Be?

Where would I be without the Lord
Abiding in my heart?
I'd have no interest in His word
And in Him have no part!

Where would I be without His love
To give me calm repose?
I'd have no treasures stored above—
No shelter from my foes!

Where would I be without His grace?
I'd still be lost in sin!
I could not run the Christian race
Nor have sweet peace within!

Where would I be without His pow'r
To keep me day by day?
I could not stand, ev'n for one hour,
For soon I'd go astray!

I'm less than nothing without Him—
Less than the least am I;
My fate would be, alas, most grim,
Without Him I would die!

Abide Thou near me, Gracious Friend,
To guide, and guard, and shield;
And till I reach my journey's end,
My all to Thee I yield.

Forevermore in Heaven's bliss
I hope to sing Thy praise!
O, what a glorious prospect, this!
To be with Thee always!

PART 5
THE HOPE OF HEAVEN

Longing to be with Christ
I long to be where Jesus is,
To realize His promises;
To be made like our glorious King,
And His eternal praises sing.

No sweeter joy could we partake
Than in His likeness to awake;
To then in Him be satisfied,
And where He is to e'er abide.

In His Bosom
With my dear Lord I wish to be,
Communing with the Trinity;
Delighting there eternally
In His great love and Deity.

What greater joy could we desire
Than in His bosom to retire?
To know as even we are known,
And ne'er again to weep or groan.

221

A House Not Made With Hands

We know not when the hour will come
When death shall stake its claim,
Upon this feeble house of clay,
This fast-decaying frame.

But blessed hope lies in our breast
That in eternity,
We'll have a house not made with hands,
From sin entirely free.

Carried to the Skies

Thou whose pow'r has been displayed
Through the heav'ns and in the earth;
Thou by whom the worlds were made,
Author of our heav'nly birth;
Keep us now by this same pow'r,
That we may Thy servants be,
Till that long-awaited hour
When we sleep in peace with Thee.
Then may we in triumph rise
From that cold and silent grave,
And be carried to the skies
E'er to sing Thy power to save.

Yet Another Dawn

How sweet the light at break of day,
And songs with which the birds awake!
With joy the grass consumes the dew;
All nature doth of heav'n partake.

But there is yet another dawn;
O how our souls doth wait the day!
When Christ returns with angels near,
And wafts His blood-bought bride away.

With tuneful strains we'll lift our voice,
More sweetly than the birds can sing;
With raptured chorus endlessly
The halls of heav'n with praise will ring.

A Bright Prospect

Dear Lord, we've sought to praise Thy name
And fondly speak of Thy good;
But our best works are stained by sin—
We can't perform as we would.

But hope springs up that one sweet day,
From sin we'll be clean and free;
No more to mourn our weakness here,
But perfectly worship Thee.

Hastening Toward Our Lord's Return
Our life is as a flickering flame—
A moment here in time;
It seems that only yesterday
Our strength was in its prime.

Our youthful years have fled apace
As though they ne'er had been;
Our pain-racked body soon must pay
The final wage of sin.

But we look toward our Lord's return—
That great grave-op'ning day;
Our bodies shall be glorified
And never more decay.

Soon to be With Christ
With dear old Abraham we say,
Our days are few and evil too;
Our lives are passing swift away—
Experience tells us it is true.

These bodies speak their swift decline;
Departure looms more near each day;
But this doth only haste the time
When we shall be with Christ to stay.

The Death of Saints

Death for the righteous is not marked
By gloomy, sad finality;
But 'tis their passage to a place
Of joy and peace eternally.

It marks the end of toil and strife,
And lifts the veil from joys untold;
It wafts the soul away to Christ
Where none shall e'er again grow old.

And in the resurrection morn,
The soul and body reunite;
And saints ascend to meet their Lord
And dwell with Him in endless light.

Longing For Heaven

All nat'ral beauty swiftly fades,
And things of earth decay;
Unholy men oft' vex our souls
By what they do and say.

These troubling scenes make us desire
A better place above;
Where all is everlasting peace,
With pure and endless love.

How Glad the Day!

Imprisoned in a house of clay,
Our steps each day more feeble grow;
The sin in Eden left its mark
And soon will lay our bodies low.

Sin's stain appears o'er all the earth,
In ev'ry evil known to man;
Its sad effects reach ev'ry heart;
It ruins lives and blights the land.

How glad the day when Jesus comes,
When sin and death are at an end,
And saints arrayed in robes of white
Will with their mighty King ascend!

God Will Have the Final Say

How sad when ev'ry evil thing
Abounds throughout our once-great land;
When false religion rules the day
And millions build upon the sand.

When Presidents and Emperors
Are ruled themselves by Satan's pow'r;
And freedoms which were once our creed
Are growing fewer by the hour.

If God were not still on the throne
Our plight would surely hopeless be;
But He will have the final say
And saints will have the victory.

A Leaning Bough

My life is like a leaning bough
That ever feels the strain;
Few are the peaceful moments when
I feel no stress nor pain.

My shadow stretches farther east
As day draws nearer night;
The bough bends nearer to the earth—
It must give up the fight.

But soon the bough will rise again,
"Twill then be evergreen;
"Twill stand with arms spread t'ward the sky,
And ne'er again shall lean.

The Death of Saints

A time most dreaded by the world—
The fearful hour of death!
No comfort shall the worldling find
When breathing his last breath.

How diff'rent is the death of saints!
How precious is that hour!
When heav'n receives their happy souls
Into that blissful bower!

Forever severed from the world,
In endless love they bask;
And find that heaven holds far more
Than e'er they could have asked.

A Day of Joy

There is a day of joy ahead
When Christ will raise us from the dead;
As sure as blood is crimson red,
Our Lord will do just what He said.

He'll come again some happy day
And waft His people all away;
With Him in heav'n they'll ever stay,
In that bright land of endless day.

Our soul and body, glorified,
Will be forever satisfied;
No tear shall e'er again be cried,
For peace and love will e'er abide.

It Won't Be Long

We'll only be on earth a while—
Our stay here won't be long;
We need to live close to the Lord,
And in His grace be strong.

Our days are few and evil too,
So let us prayerful be;
It won't be long till Jesus comes,
And then we will be free.

Our warfare soon will have an end,
And then eternal peace
Shall fill our happy soul and heart,
And joy will never cease.

I'll Gladly Go

So many things disturb my peace
In this old world of sin;
I often bow my head and ask,
When will it have an end?

'Tis good to know a better place
Awaits us by and by;
Where there will be no further pain
And none will ever die.

Till then I'll strive to be resigned
To God's own will and mind;
And when He calls I'll gladly go
And leave this world behind.

Rejoice With Me

When death shall claim this mortal frame
And lay me 'neath the cov'ring sod;
Rejoice with me, ye who remain,
That I am with my Savior God.

Your tears will show your tender love,
But don't allow them long to flow;
For I will be well satisfied
In that bright land to which I go.

On earth I've known much pain and grief,
And oft my sins have bent me low;
But heav'n will bring a sweet relief,
And there will be no further woe.

Heaven

Eternal joy, incessant peace
In heav'n will be our lot;
And all the grief we've known down here,
Will there all be forgot.

Communion with our precious Lord,
Unbroken, there will be;
And no distractions can disturb
That pure tranquility.

The millions there will ne'er divide,
And none shall e'er offend;
And perfect union, love and praise
Will never, never end.

That's Where I Hope to Go

There is a perfect, peaceful place
With not a frown on any face,
Of grief there's not the slightest trace;
That's where I hope to go!

The saints will all be gathered 'round,
And joy and peace will e'er abound,
For no distress can there be found;
That's where I hope to go!

No tears up there will e'er be shed,
There'll be no fear, there'll be no dread;
And when I'm numbered with the dead,
That's where I hope to go!

Victory in Christ
O grave, where is thy victory?
O death, where is thy sting?
In view of what our Lord has done,
No ruin canst thou bring.

Thou art a pale, defeated foe,
A serpent well defanged;
A bear whose teeth have been removed,
A roaring lion chained.

The saints shall die in living faith
And come forth from the grave;
Triumphant through their risen Lord,
For e'er His name to praise.

No Parting There
God's people ne'er shall say farewell,
To never meet again;
At last they'll meet in heav'nly bliss,
With Christ for e'er to reign.

Though they may part to meet no more
Upon the shores of time,
Yet all at last shall reunite
In happy realms sublime.

Our partings here oft times give pain,
And tears flow freely down;
But when in heaven we'll part no more
And joy shall e'er abound.

Holy Ground

Dreary days are turned to singing
When the Spirit fills our breast;
Then with heart to Jesus clinging,
We find blessed peace and rest.

While we walk in His approval,
We enjoy His warm embrace;
And we wait for our removal
To a far more happy place.

When at last we are a'dying,
And our loved ones gather round;
Let them cease their mournful sighing,
For we're nearing holy ground.

A Happy Place

There is a happy, peaceful place
Awaiting ev'ry saint;
Where there will be no pain or tears,
Nor ever a complaint.

That lofty place will brim with joy,
And none can e'er be sad;
The souls of all, once entered there,
Will ever more be glad.

Our Lord arrayed in robes of white
Will captivate each heart;
And from His presence pure and bright,
No one shall e'er depart.

Looking for a Better Land
This is a dark and evil world
That we are passing through;
And imperfections, change and sin,
Are stamped on all we do.

This present world is not our home—
We're strangers here below;
We're looking for a better land,
Where joys forever flow.

That city far beyond the stars
Looms shortly up ahead;
Where we expect with great delight
To see our Living Head.

How Sweet 'Twill Be
What awful pain I've oft endured
Throughout my sojourn here!
How sweet 'twill be that happy place
Where ne'er is shed a tear!

What awful grief I oft have felt
When Satan has assailed!
How sweet 'twill be when I at last
Have o'er all grief prevailed!

What trouble sore my soul has known
But soon 'twill all be o'er!
No pain, no grief, no trouble sore,
But piece forevermore!

An End to Sorrow

Soon our journey will be over
And we'll pass this way no more;
Pain and suffering will be ended
And all sorrow will be o'er.

Ne'er will hurtful words be spoken;
Ne'er will friends become our foes;
Ne'er will hearts be rent and broken;
Ne'er will joys be turned to woes.

Then our peace will be eternal
With the saints of God above;
Thus in place of grief and sorrow,
Will be endless joy and love.

Heaven is Always Serene

The hordes are dashing to and fro
Here midst these scenes of sin and woe;
Turmoil and chaos oft are seen,
Yet, heaven always is serene.

Great dashing billows 'round us roar,
And oft we're faced with grief galore;
Much fear is seen on many a face,
Yet, heav'n remains a peaceful place.

No lasting peace shall here be known,
And life will call forth many a groan;
Till death there'll be much to annoy,
But, heav'n will always be a joy.

Joy Unspeakable

Though we have never seen the Lord
With these our fleshly eyes,
Yet we believe and so rejoice
And sweetly realize...
Joy unspeakable
And full of glory.

We hope to see Him face to face
In just a little while,
When we are wafted to the skies
And enter with a smile...
Joy unspeakable
And full of glory.

Perfect Rest

Dear Gracious God, I often find
My stubborn will opposed to Thine;
And when I would do good I see
An evil nature lives in me.

Its ugly head it raises up,
And I thus drink a bitter cup
Of sadness and of deep regret,
Which makes me often groan and fret

One day I hope to lay it down
And leave it burned up in the ground;
When I arise with glory dressed,
And live with Thee in perfect rest.

That Bright City

When I with Christ arise
And up to heaven soar,
With sin I'll ever more be done
And wish for earth no more.

The Lord will be our light
With radiant beauty there;
We'll no more need earth's candle-glow
In that bright city fair.

No darkness there can come,
But glory e'er will shine;
No gloom can cloud the pleasure of
Eternal light Divine.

Then We'll Know

O, who can tell the wonder of
Our great Redeemer's endless love;
Or who by search can amply trace
The boundaries of His wondrous grace?

Who, by the closest of exam,
Can fully know the Great I AM?
What eye can peer into His heart?
For now we only know in part.

One day we'll better understand
As we ascend to Glory Land,
When Jesus comes to claim His own,
And then we'll know as we are known.

After Death

The righteous, when he dies,
Is carried to the skies,
Where joys forevermore
Are his to e'er explore.

The wicked, when he dies,
For e'er in mis'ry lies;
His pleasures all then cease
And ne'er does he know peace.

But blest are all who die
With hearts to God drawn nigh;
For there shall they abide,
Forever satisfied!

Heaven's Joys

I live in hope of heaven's joys—
Its beauties can't be told;
I've long grown tired of earthly toys,
I covet not its gold.

That land of rest beyond this vale
Can never fade away;
Compared to it earth's joys are pale,
And soon they all decay.

I lay not up my treasures here
Where moth and rust destroy;
But in that happy land of cheer
Where naught can e'er annoy.

No More Conflicts

There are flowers in the desert,
There are comforts amid pain,
There are rainbows to remind us
That our Master rules the rain.

There are roses in the thorn-bush,
And there's hope where all seems lost;
There are blessings in afflictions,
So we humbly bear the cost.

There's an upside and a downside
To this life down here below;
But there'll ne'er be any conflicts
In that land to which we go.

A Stranger Here I Feel To Be[1]

I care not for this world of sin,
I seek a better land;
A country far above the skies
With all the chosen band.

The spoils of earth have lost their glow,
Their emptiness is plain;
The sins which draw the carnal mind
Afford me nought but pain.

That which appeals to flesh and blood
Is vexing to my soul;
And that which I desire the least,
The world sets as its goal.

---

[1] Previously published in *The Baptist Witness*, January 1986. Used by permission.

'Tis hard to find an earthly friend
On whom we can rely;
One who will truly take a stand
And for the truth would die.

A stranger here I feel to be,
I long to fly away;
To live in peace with Christ our Lord
In perfect, endless day.

I'll be no stranger in that land;
At home I'll ever be,
Where bitter tears have taken wings
And saints at last are free.

We've Passed This Way[2]

We've passed this way,
Conceived in sin;
Bound up with trials,
Our days have been.

We've passed this way,
But soon will leave,
And go where none,
Shall ever grieve.

We've passed this way,
We've prayed, we've sung,
And praised God's name,
With heart and tongue.

---

[2] Previously published in *The Christian Pathway*, April 1991. Used by permission.

We've passed this way,
And known God's love,
And hope at last,
To rest above.

We've passed this way,
We've suffered grief,
And learned with time,
That life is brief.

We've passed this way,
'Twill soon be o'er;
Then pain and grief,
Will be no more.

This House of Clay[3]

This house of clay grows weaker now
From long exposure and decay;
It soon shall crumble back to earth,
It never was designed to stay.

But on the resurrection morn,
It shall be raised to life and peace;
And then it can no more decay,
Its joys with God will never cease.

Clothed in His perfect righteousness,
It shall fore'er remain the same;
With undiminished strength and love,
'Twill joyously adore His name.

---

[3] Previously published in *The Christian Pathway*, May 1993. Used by permission.

Its timbers shall not shake with fear;
'Twill revel in eternal bliss;
Its halls will ring with endless praise,
O, what a blessed hope is this!

It Will Be Me

Though once a microscopic sperm,
No bigger than a tiny germ,
Too small for human eye to see,
It still was life, and it was me.

Abortion did not still my breath;
I was preserved from infant death.
I was a child, and then a man,
Kept by a gracious, sovereign hand.

With time my feeble breath must cease,
To God my soul shall go in peace;
My body in the grave shall stay
Until the resurrection day.

And when the Lord returns in light,
My soul and flesh shall re-unite,
To dwell with Him eternally,
And praise His name—it will be me.

Forever Satisfied

In heav'n there'll be no heartache,
No sorrow, grief or pain;
No storm-clouds there will gather,
There'll be no wind or rain.

There'll be no cold of Winter,
Nor heat of Summer's sun;
No calloused hand from toiling,
Nor wickedness to shun.

There'll be no burning fever,
No walking-cane or crutch,
No dread disease like cancer,
No withered limbs and such.

There'll be no wars or strivings,
No shots will e'er be fired;
There'll be no death nor dying,
And none will e'er grow tired.

There'll be no interruptions,
Of worship or of joy;
There'll be no imperfection,
And nothing to annoy.

We'll be like Christ our Savior,
With Him we'll e'er abide;
We'll dwell in peaceful splendor,
Forever satisfied.

The Battle is Over[4]

Another dear old soldier-saint
Has fought the battle well,
And now has gained the victory
O'er Satan, death and hell.

The house of clay in which she dwelt
Will molder back to dust;
But now her soul is with the Lord
In whom was all her trust.

Our precious Savior soon will come
Her sleeping dust to raise,
With all the other saints of God
Fore'er to sing His praise.

In spirit she is far removed
Beyond all pain and strife;
To ne'er again be laden with
The troubles of this life.

May we then sweetly bid farewell
And grieve and mourn no more;
For she doth now with angels dwell
On Heaven's blissful shore.

---

[4] Composed upon the occasion of the death of Mable Wells, the author's aunt, and adapted by Elder Louis Culver for publication in the June 1993 edition of *In The Master's Service*, as an appendix to the obituary of H. T. Rimmer, a beloved member of New Harmony Primitive Baptist Church, Clanton, Alabama.

Another Friend Has Gone[5]

Another friend has gone away
Unto the land of endless day;
Her raptured soul has taken flight,
Ascending to the realms of light.

She now with saints unites to sing
The praises of her God and King;
No pain disturbs that blood-washed throng;
No sour note distorts their song.

The pain she knew while here she dwelt
Cannot in glory e'er be felt;
The grief that marred her earthly stay
Is now forever done away.

If we could only glimpse her state,
What joy in us it would create!
The smallest view of her domain
Would drive away our ev'ry pain.

Let us recall with fondest thought
The good that here on earth she wrought;
Her good examples emulate
While now, by faith, we watch and wait.

She would not have us much to grieve
But would our tears with joy relieve;
Her self-less spirit would behest,
"Rejoice in God, who gave me rest."

Then may we not in sorrow grope,
Nor grieve as those who have no hope [1 Ths. 4:13]
But may our all on God be cast
And hope to join our friend at last.

---

[5] Composed upon the death of Mrs. Margie Simmons, the oldest daughter of the author's Aunt Mable Wells. Her body was laid to rest in the cemetery at Bethel Primitive Baptist Church, near Bonifay, Fla., Dec. 28, 1989, beside the place her mother would lay two and one half years later.

A Solemn Bequeathal of a Lady[6]

We now bequeath this clay to dust,
From whence to rise, (one day it must)
Adorned with righteousness Divine,
Bedecked with glory, pure, sublime.

Eternity, that vast unknown,
Now swallows up her ev'ry groan;
Enwraps her soul in endless bliss
And greets her with celestial kiss.

A newly-welcomed guest above
Now basks in her dear Savior's love;
And though, for now, with her we part,
Her mem'ry lingers in our heart.

Submissively we view this tomb,
For soon from thence this dust will come;
May we rejoice with her as we
Commit her spirit, Lord, to Thee.

Memory's Book

From birth the time is brief till we
Begin to speak of former years;
A checkered past soon writes a page
Which often draws reflective peers.

The picture that the book portrays
Doth to our mem'ry oft appear;
Sometimes it calls for thankful praise,
But other times it brings a tear.

---

[6] Ibid.

We fondly wait that blissful day
When mem'ry's book will be wiped clear,
Of all that caused us grief or pain
And brought to life the bitter tear.

The only mem'ries we shall know
In heaven's hallowed atmosphere,
Are those which bring us sweet delight
And make our view of Christ more dear.

In Heaven

In heav'n there'll be no tear-dimmed eyes,
No shocking scenes nor sad surprise,
No dread disease nor growing old,
No storms and floods, no heat or cold.

There'll be no thieves nor liars there,
No obscene language anywhere;
No liquor stores, no ruined lives,
No broken homes nor beaten wives.

No economic wants or woes,
No threat of war from evil foes,
No worried minds nor sleepless nights,
No cloudy skies, no fears nor frights.

No feeble minds, no failing sight,
No ruined fields from drought or blight,
No death or dying over there,
No hint of heartache, pain or care.

No wickedness of any kind,
No one who's crippled, deaf or blind,
No Tempter to disturb the joy,
No evil spirit to annoy.

All will be sweet and perfect peace;
The pleasures there will never cease;
With Christ the saints will e'er abide,
Filled with delight and satisfied.

Time hastens on, it won't be long,
I'm nearing that eternal home;
O joyful land, so bright and fair,
My soul is longing to be there!

The Lord's Coming[7]

While we are bound in frames of clay,
Heav'n doth appear unclearly;
And in this dark and gloomy day,
We cling to hope most dearly.

Our Lord will soon appear,
Though when is now unclear;
Till then we pray for grace
To run the Christian race,
While we await His coming.

The promise of His soon return
Doth keep us ever striving,
To be found faithful—thus to yearn
The day of His arriving.

---

[7] This hymn-poem may be sung to the tune of "A Mighty Fortress is Our God."

O may our songs be raised,
With anthems filled with praise,
And may we view with cheer
What evil men now fear,
And gladly wait His coming.

That day will dawn with splendor great
Beyond all comprehension;
And none can hide behind the guise
Of all their false pretension.

The veil shall fall away
From ev'ry evil way,
And nothing but the pure
Will in that hour endure,
As we behold His coming.

No More Sin

How bitter, Lord, have been the tears
We've shed because of sin;
And Oh, how blest will be the day
This grief will have an end!

Transgression has no place in heav'n,
Sin cannot there draw near;
The saints will no more feel its curse
Nor shed another tear.

By virtue of Thy precious blood
And perfect righteousness,
Thy people stand before Thee pure,
Arrayed in royal dress.

When We Reach Our Home in Glory

When we reach our home in Glory
What a happy time 'twill be!
All our troubles will be ended
And our Savior we shall see.

All adorned in His perfection,
Voices all attuned as one;
We'll behold His wondrous beauty
Shining brighter than the sun.

There our voices will be blended
As we've never sung before;
And our hearts will thrill forever
As our Savior we adore.

All our fondest dreams of Heaven
Will be far exceeded there;
We'll be free from all temptation,
Ne'er a sorrow, pain nor tear.

No distressing thought to grieve us,
There will be no sad goodbyes;
All our hearts will be united
In that home beyond the skies.

Joy which passeth understanding
Shall be seen in ev'ry eye;
All the saints will shout together
And they never more shall die.

Blessed, sweet anticipation!
Wistful hearts await the day;
In a cloud of heav'nly glory
They'll be carried home to stay.

When the glory land we enter,
This our constant song will be,
"Thou art worthy, blest Redeemer,
All our praises to receive."

No More Tears

A flood of sad and bitter tears
O'er wasted years are shed,
And many weep because of fears
Of what may lie ahead.

The tears of num'rous souls are traced
To teachings false and vain;
They do not know God's wondrous grace
And cannot trust the same.

Tears are a very common thing
Among the sons of men;
Great tears from unkind words that sting
And ev'ry form of sin.

A host of tears are shed in grief
O'er loved ones in the tomb,
And others rise from unbelief
Which breeds a hopeless gloom.

Great numbers weep because men cry
That heaven must be won
By ev'rything beneath the sky,
Except what Christ has done.

They labor hard to measure up
To standards they can't reach;
And often find a bitter cup
In things false prophets preach.

A thousand things on earth bring tears,
But there will come a day
When Christ in glor'ous light appears
To wipe our tears away.

The saints will never weep again,
There'll be no further fears;
There'll be no further grief or pain,
And there'll be no more tears.

How Blest They Are

How blest are they whom God hath loved,
Whose home in heav'n is fixed;
Who know the gospel and in whom
The word with faith is mixed!

How safely do they rest in Christ
Secure in cov'nant love!
Their treasure is not earthly but
Is safely housed above.

How happy are they when they feel
The presence of their King!
And how delightful when with joy
Their soul is blest to sing!

How blest are they to know and love
The gospel's joyful sound,
And thus to be assured by faith
That they are heaven bound!

How blest are they to be sustained
By grace from day to day;
And ev'ry mom to wake assured
That grace will lead the way!

How blest are they to be a child
Of God's amazing grace;
And thus to have the privilege
To run the Christian race!

How blest are they to have a hope
Of happiness ahead,
When Christ returns with trumpet sound
And raises all the dead!

How blest indeed when saints arise
To mansions in the sky!
How blest to ever be with Christ
Where none will ever die!

An Endless Day

My soul awaits the day
When I am called away
From all the sorrows of this life
Unto an endless day.

How happy we shall be
When Jesus we shall see!
And there arrayed in robes of white,
From sin we shall be free.

No grief shall e'er molest
That endless day of rest;
And all who reach that happy home
Shall be forever blest.

The joys that shall be there
With earth cannot compare;
And peace will reign forevermore
In that sweet home so fair.

In heaven none can die,
Or breathe the faintest sigh;
For all is perfect in that land
Of bliss and peace on high.

The pleasures of God's grace
No tear shall e'er erase;
And what a joy it e'er shall be
To look upon His face!

While here on earth we stay,
May we by grace display—
The love of Christ within our hearts
By serving Him each day.

Looking Forward to the Morning

There is much on earth to grieve us
And extort from us a groan;
But relief will come tomorrow
As we travel further on.

Our own hearts will oft deceive us
While in sinful flesh we dwell;
But we have the sweet assurance,
"With the righteous it is well."

Friends may sometimes plunge a dagger
To the depths of our poor soul;
But one loving smile from Jesus
And our wounds are all made whole.

We may find ourselves desponding
'Neath the world's relentless frown;
But the Lord will in His mercy
Place our feet on higher ground.

Sin will never cease to plague us
While we're dwelling here below;
But no sin can ever enter
That bright land to which we go.

Satan tries His best to have us
And to sift us day by day;
But from him and all his demons
We will one day fly away.

Let us rest, then, in the promise
Of a home beyond the skies;
And look forward to the morning
When with Christ we shall arise.

Our Sojourn Here

A while on earth will make us glad
To leave these mundane scenes behind;
So many things here make us sad,
The thought of heav'n oft' fills our mind.

Vile though we are in nature's blood,
Our hope in Christ doth yet endure;
Though sin enshrouds us like a flood,
His mercy keeps us still secure.

Temptations rage on ev'ry hand
And oft we're backward to resist;
But by his grace we still yet stand
And all his graces we enlist.

Without His mercies we would fall,
And of this truth there is no doubt;
We must on Him relentless call
Or face a soul-distressing drought.

Our sojourn on the shores of time
Was never meant to be carefree;
No heights are reached without a climb—
No joys without a bended knee.

We struggle here from day to day
And meet the foe on ev'ry hand,
Not daring e'er to cease to pray
Till we ascend to Glory Land.

Till then, Dear Father, be our guide,
And keep us in the narrow way;
And then when heaven's gate swings wide
Receive us into endless day.

Vast Glories

How vast Thy glories, Lord, Most High!
They reach beyond this nether sky,
To regions where no craft can go,
To depths we mortals cannot know.

How vast the powers of Thy mind!
No force can turn, no hand can bind;
Thou canst but speak and it is done,
No pow'r can vie with Thee—not one.

How vast the tokens of Thy grace,
Thy loving smiles, Thy warm embrace!
For these we praise Thee and adore
And long for grace to love Thee more.

How vast the works that Thou hast wrought!
Not one has ever come to naught;
Thy purpose must forever stand,
For none can stay Thy mighty hand.

How vast the scope of Thy great love
Both here and in the realms above;
Embracing millions far and near
And cheering hearts with comforts dear!

How vast the mercies Thou hast giv'n
To Thy beloved heirs of heav'n!
What glories yet remain ahead
When we are brought up from the dead!

How vast the joys we then shall know
When toils are ended here below!
How vast the pleasure, vast the peace,
And praises there that never cease!

O Land of Everlasting Joy
No tears e'er fall in Heaven's courts,
No sigh is ever heard;
There are no cries of anguish there
And ne'er an unkind word.

There always is a tranquil air,
An everlasting joy;
Contentment reigns eternal there
And nothing can annoy.

The glory of our Savior God
Lights up that City Fair;
And songs of praise ring sweet and pure,
His wonders to declare.

The occupants of that bright land
Are ever satisfied;
Delighted to be settled there,
And there to e'er abide.

The wondrous peace that fills that place
On earth was never known;
But only foretastes, briefly giv'n,
When special grace was shown.

But there the heavenly joys proceed
With naught to interfere;
All hearts are ever tuned to sing
And Christ is always near.

I'm waiting here, O gracious Lord,
Confined to sin-cursed ground;
O take me soon to be with Thee
Where peace doth e'er abound.

Time and Eternity[8]

The with'ring joys of earth
Are not to be compared,
With everlasting joys of heaven
Which Jesus hath prepared.

These present temp'ral scenes—
How fleeting and unsure!
But things eternal never fade;
They always will endure.

There is a yearning deep
Within our longing heart;
A better place to ever dwell
And from all strife to part.

Sometimes it seems that we
A glimpse of heav'n can see;
And if we could we'd fly away
From sin to e'er be free.

The fleeting hours of time
Are nothing when we think
Of ceaseless ages which endure
Beyond the river's brink.

The pain, the grief, the strife,
They all will cease to be,
When, gathered 'round the throne, the saints
Shall sing eternally.

Then blow, ye winds of earth,
And waft us quickly o'er
The stormy seas to that peace-land,
To praise God ever more.

---

[8] Stanzas 1 and 5-7 by George R. Bretz (1912); Stanzas 2-4 by Ralph E. Harris (2004).

No Scoffers in Heaven

The distant regions of the stars,
Unmeasured and unknown,
Are nestled in God's mighty hand
And are His work alone.

Men peer through glasses at the skies
To search this vast expanse,
And reason in their darkened mind—
"It came about by chance."

But purpose does not blend with chance:
God works and none can stay
His mighty hand of providence
Nor wish His works away.

His great creation e'er shall stand
Till He with it is done;
And then He'll have no further use
For earth or moon or sun.

Then all the elements will burn
And melt with fervent heat,
While all the saints are safe at home,
No more with grief to meet.

The scoffers will be cast away
To their appointed place,
While saints rejoice in their dear Lord
And look upon His face.

There they shall ever praise His name
And none shall e'er molest;
And there will never be an end
To that sweet home of rest.

Happy Place! O Happy Place!

When I contemplate the things the Scriptures say,
I'm reminded of how oft' I disobey;
I'm a sinner, and by nature I am vile,
Yet I live in hope that I'm a re-born child.

Oft' my pathway is beset with gins and snares
And I watch lest I be taken unawares;
Safety lies in Christ the Lord, my All in All,
And apart from His protection I must fall.

Many times I find myself out of the way,
And my wandering thoughts are often gone astray;
How I need the Lord to keep my feet aright
That with courage I may wage a noble fight.

How delightful are the hours when He is near,
And the way ahead seems brighter and more clear!
How I long to be with Him for e'er above
Where there's never-ending peace, and joy, and love!

Temporal wealth cannot provide a moment's peace,
Nor from evils and temptations give release;
But in death I'll leave all worldly things behind,
And in heaven I'll find treasures all divine.

There with saints long gone from earth I'll sweetly dwell
And with angels I shall sing that "all is well;"
"Satisfied" will be the state of every heart
And we ne'er again will from the Lord depart.

Happy place! O happy place! I long for thee!
And I wonder when the call will come for me;
May the Lord direct my steps until that day,
When with joy beyond compare I fly away.

Hold Fast

As we observe the passing years
And see how swift they fly,
We know 'twill be but just awhile
'Till we are called to die.

The Lord will give a grand discharge
From ev'ry temp'ral thing;
And take us to His sweet abode
Where endless praises ring.

But 'till that day may we hold fast
Our great profession dear,
And ever look with dauntless faith
For Jesus to appear.

⚜

Divine Things Worth Far More

One tiny grain of grace Divine
Is surely worth far more
Than all the gold men might amass
Upon a timely shore.

One spark of light from God's own hand
Possesses far more worth
Than all the learning secular
Existing on the earth.

One moment of the bliss above
And all the saints might say,
"No joy of earth can e'er compare
With sweet eternal day."

Hope Most Precious[9]
Hope, most precious in the storms
Of life's raging sea,
Is an anchor to my soul,
Speaking peace to me;
Speaking peace to me,
Of my Lord and King;
Hope dispels my sorrow,
Speaking peace to me.

Hope, tho' worthless to the blind,
Is a solid stay
To the trembling child of grace,
Struggling on his way;
Struggling on his way,
Toiling ev'ry day;
To the weary pilgrim,
Struggling on his way.

Hope, when unbelief is strong
And temptation sore,
Keeps us ever pressing on
T'ward the blissful shore;
T'ward the blissful shore,
Where we'll die no more;
Hope, our guide and compass,
T'ward the blissful shore.

Hope of heaven's sinless clime
Is a prospect dear,
And can never be compared
To our sorrows here;

To our sorrows here,
Fleeting pain and care;
These cannot compare with
Endless glories there.

PART 6
GODLY LIVING

The Way of Peace
Dear children of the Lord,
Hold fast to truth and right,
Departing not from Him,
But walking in the light.

For in this way is peace
The world knows nothing of,
Bringing this assurance—
We share in God's great love.

The Narrow Way
The narrow way that leads to life
Is fraught with fiery trials;
And few the faithful trav'lers there
Who brave the tempter's wiles.

Rejoice! Rejoice! Ye blessed saints
Who walk this hallowed way;
Thy Savior says thy strength shall be
Sufficient for thy day.

Lifeless Charms

O, dost thou have a favored sin
Thou loathest to forsake;
An idol hidden in thy tent?
Oh! what a sad mistake!

Cast out these deadly, lifeless charms,
And tear them from their throne;
All real and lasting joy is found
In godliness alone.

Sowing and Reaping

Dear child of God, dost thou not know
That thou shalt reap what thou dost sow?
If to thy flesh thou sow'st thy fields,
Corruption is the fruit it yields.

And if thou sparingly shall sow,
Then sparingly thy fruits shall grow;
But if abundant seeds are sown,
Abundant fruit shall then be grown.

May Jesus help thee sow good seeds
In all thy tho'ts, and words, and deeds;
And thou shalt find in harvest days,
It shall return in num'rous ways.

Opposing Principles

One cannot find much sympathy
Where haughtiness is known;
Compassion is a rarity
Where pride is on the throne.

Humility of godly sort
Can't co-exist with pride,
And Christian love cannot resort
Where hatred doth reside.

O purge away our dross, dear Lord,
And purify each part,
That we may love and serve Thee from
A good and honest heart.

Narrow is the Way

Strait is the gate that leads to life—
Few find its narrow way;
But sure destruction's path is broad
And many therein stray.

There is a way that seemeth right
To Adam's fallen seed;
But multitudes at last shall find,
To ruin it doth lead.

The narrow way is where we find
The humble souls who pray;
O may we walk with these dear ones
And with the Lord each day!

Show Me the Footprints

Show me the footprints of the flock
And where at noon they rest;
Show me the way the world rejects,
By heaven owned and blest.

Show me that humble, trusting way,
The world calls heresy;
'Tis there I long to walk and live;
Its joys are rich and free.

And then at last when Christ returns
To raise and claim His own,
No man need show me anymore,
I'll know as I am known.

Noble Men

The noblest men I've ever known,
Were men of humble heart;
They would not compromise the truth,
Nor alter any part.

Their chief desire, and highest aim,
Was keeping God's command;
And with the Cause of Christ at stake,
They dared to take a stand.

O give us more such men, dear Lord,
Men meek and mild, yet stern,
To bravely stand for truth and right,
Until Thou dost return.

Whatever It Takes

Whate'er it takes, O gracious Lord,
To keep me at Thy feet;
For Thee I'll bear the beggars lot,
And fill the pauper's seat.

If I must suffer grief or pain,
That I may humble be,
Then I will gladly suffer, Lord,
But kindly stand by me.

Whate'er it takes to keep me low
And useful in Thy sight,
If Thou wilt only be my strength
And give me grace and light.

The Christian Life

How careful must the Christian be!
How chaste in life and lip!
For he attracts the critic's gaze,
Who watches ev'ry slip.

The world thinks little of the saint
But much of him expect;
They profit by his godly life,
But godliness reject.

O saint of God, "quit ye like men,"
In Christian armor dressed;
We shall at last o'ercome the world
And find eternal rest.

Immortal Treasures

Thy word, dear Lord, with promise sweet
Doth to the righteous say,
That Thou wilt give sufficient grace
To hold them on their way.

No worthwhile thing wilt Thou withhold
From those who walk upright;
They shall be filled with holy zeal
And bathed in heav'nly light.

Immortal treasures, joy untold,
And love beyond degree;
Such are the pleasures Thou dost give
To those who follow Thee.

To God Be True

Be kind to all thy fellow men,
For God is kind to you;
And leave all vengeance in *His* hand
No matter what *they* do.

Be good to all who cross thy path,
For God is good to you;
Remember where you used to be,
And where He brought you, too.

Bear long with those who're close to thee,
For God bears long with you;
No matter where your path may lead,
To Him be ever true.

May God Be Glorified
May we let our light shine brightly
That our works, both true and tried,
May be seen by those around us
And our God be glorified.

And when tempted to seek vengeance,
Humbly lay all wrath aside;
Follow Christ and His example
And He will be glorified.

May we strive to be like Jesus,
In His love to e'er abide;
So that we may feel when dying,
His great name we've glorified.

*

Ask Yourself
When ill of others you might speak,
Take a while to think it through;
Consider this one question first,
Would you want it said of you?

'Ere you do a thing to others,
Pause a while and think it through;
Would you wish to be thus treated?
Would you want it done to you?

In such matters make these queries,
Is it right? and, Is it true?
Then to self propose this question,
Would you want it done to you?

*

The Golden Rule

"Do unto others as you would
That they should do to you;"
This is indeed a golden rule—
A rule we should pursue.

O how much better world we'd have
If men this rule obeyed;
All war would cease, all strife would end,
And none would be afraid!

O may we strive each day anew
To heed this great command;
And thus we shall be recognized
As heirs of Glory Land!

Real and Lasting Wealth

If men should gain the entire world,
What would it profit them,
If they should be found out of Christ
And have no part in Him?

We should not worship worldly goods,
All such will one day burn;
In death we'll leave them all behind
And to them ne'er return.

The only real and lasting wealth
Is what we have above;
And all we'll ever really need
Is God's eternal love.

Turn Not Away

When Israel turned away from God,
They groaned beneath His chast'ning rod;
And thus it is with us today,
We suffer when we turn away.

The Lord says, "Come to me for rest
And ye shall be most richly blest;"
But multitudes reject His word
And seem as though they never heard.

The only way we'll ever know
The joy of service here below,
Is to obey with fervent love
And set our hearts on things above.

Treat Others Kindly

If to others I am friendly,
Others then my friends will be;
But if I no kindness show them,
Then will they show none to me.

How we treat our fellow soldiers
Much determines how we feel;
Peace of conscience is a treasure
None can borrow, beg nor steal.

May we build a reputation
Tarnished not by friend or foe,
So that when our jouney's over,
Friends will loath to see us go.

Watch Your Tongue
The fires of hell are set ablaze
By tongues turned loose to wag;
Such tongues will often deal in lies
And oft' will boast and brag.

Unbridled tongues oft cut and slash
And cause poor hearts to bleed;
How many lives have been destroyed
By tongues that sowed vile seed?

A small but mighty member 'tis,
This tongue between our cheeks;
How careful ought we all to be
Of what this member speaks!

Let Us Lean on Jesus
Many are the dangers 'round us,
Many are the schemes of men;
Thus we should be ever watchful
To evade the snares of sin.

Many are the world's allurements,
Ever seeking to ensnare;
Thus we need to keep a vigil,
Ever seeking God in prayer.

Satan's tactics are malicious
And our flesh is very weak;
Let us lean, therefore, on Jesus
And His mercy often seek.

Adorning the Doctrine

Christ has died for our transgression,
Who again by Him are born;
Let us make a good profession
And His doctrine thus adorn.

He hath borne our griefs and sorrows,
And hath kept us by His pow'r;
Thus may we through our tomorrows
Love and serve Him ev'ry hour.

From the grave He hath arisen,
Thus we likewise shall arise;
Breaking from this earthly prison,
We shall meet Him in the skies.

My Heart's Desire

From all that's sinful, all that's vain,
May I with true resolve refrain;
And by an eye of faith pursue
The things my Lord has bid me do.

I seek not worldly wealth or fame,
But would extol my Savior's name;
'Tis He alone my heart desires,
And to this end my soul aspires.

From earth one day I hope to fly
To regions far beyond the sky,
And e'er to dwell with Him in peace
Where blissful pleasures never cease.

The True Riches

O, sons of God what wealth is thine!
Joint-heirs with Christ thou art—
Of His redeemed and pardoned line,
Thou art a precious part.

Love not the ore of earthly mines
Nor lust for carnal gain;
But seek the wealth of things divine,
That ne'er is sought in vain.

Lay up in heaven thy treasures where
They cannot rust away—
Thieves cannot take thy treasures there,
And there is no decay.

How Would We Do?

When bravely martyrs faced their foes,
They so disdained their threatened woes;
They much preferred to freely die
Than their dear Lord to e'er deny.

How would we do if in their place?
Would we be brave? Would we find grace?
Would we be blest to praise God's name
While being tortured in the flame?

We may not ever face such plight,
But let us live for truth and right;
And for the saints lay down our lives
Until our "Rising-Day" arrives.

Vain Pride

Pride goes before destruction.
In Proverbs thus we read;
O pride, what rank rebellion!
Let rebels now take heed.

All those with haughty spirits
Are headed for a fall ,
While those with humble spirits
Are saved from pride and gall.

May God look down in mercy
Upon the sanctified;
And keep them from the evil
Of haughtiness and pride.

All Flesh is Grass (Isaiah 40:6)

How quickly does our body fail,
Here long we cannot stay;
Our temp'ral life takes rapid wings
And we soon fade away.

A vapor'ous life is this on earth,
Like grass we wilt and die;
We should not plant our hopes on sand,
For this shall shortly fly.

Lay up thy treasures far above
This present fleeting day;
For these shall stand when earth dissolves
And saints are caught away.

The Most Exalted Seat

I've ne'er been classed among the great,
Nor have I wished to be;
I only wish to meekly serve
My Lord with dignity.

I'll ne'er attain to worldly fame,
Nor is that my desire;
I only wish to walk with God—
No honor could be higher.

If I at last am raised to meet
My Savior in the skies,
That is the most exalted seat
A soul can realize.

Would'st Thou Follow the Lord?[1]

O dear child of the Lord,
Would'st thou follow His ways?
Would'st thou spend and be spent
In His worship and praise?

Would'st thou pay earnest heed
To the things thou hast heard,
Lest thou ever let slip
Any part of His word?

Would'st thou stand firm and true
In the Cause of the King,
Bearing all the reproach
Thy steadfastness must bring?

---

[1] Previously published in *The Baptist Witness*, March 1985. Used by permission.

Then thou faithful must be
Through the storm, flood and fire,
Ever trusting in Him
As thy chiefest desire.

It is only in Him
That the battle is won;
Not by strength nor by might,
Nor the good thou hast done.

There will be times of doubt
When the way seems unclear;
But in time clouds will fade
And the light reappear.

Trials and sorrows will come
And the foe will assail;
But with God on thy side
Thou at last shall prevail.

An Endless Store of Grace[2]
With every wayward step we take,
Some priceless ground is lost;
No pleasure that we gain from sin
Is ever worth the cost.

But when with Christ our steps agree,
Our losses are our gain,
For all those things we sacrifice
Had only brought us pain.

---

[2] Previously published in *The Baptist Witness*, April 1990. Used by permission.

"Religion never was designed
To make our pleasures less;"
True joy is found in Christ alone
And in His righteousness.

The life of faith has great reward
(A taste of heav'n below);
The more we use what God has giv'n
The more He'll make it grow.

We never can exhaust His grace,
There is an endless store;
And when we use it to His praise
He smiles, and gives us more.

Debtors to Christ[3]
How much do we owe to the Lord our Redeemer?
How much have we given in service and love?
How much would we have if we had what we've given?
How many treasures have we stored up above?

We owe all we have, and our service is meager,
And our love has not flamed as much as it should;
In giving we've fallen far short of our Savior,
And not laid up treasures as much as we could.

Help Me to Serve
O let me be Thy servant, Lord,
A lover of Thy Cause;
Not moved by evil threatenings
Nor swayed by man's applause!

---

[3] Previously published in *The Pathway of Truth*, November 1990. Used by permission.

O let me be a builder, Lord,
Who ne'er divides the flock!
Let me not lead Thy saints astray
But point them to The Rock.

Help me to labor for their good
And never faint nor fall.
O let me serve with holy zeal
Until Thy final call!

The First Psalm

Blest is the humble man of God
Who walketh not in sin;
Nor in the low, ungodly schemes
Of vile and wretched men.

His soul finds its most pure delight
In God's most holy way;
And in His law doth meditate
And live both night and day.

He shall be like a living tree,
A planting firm and strong;
Beside the river's copious tide,
His roots grow deep and long.

In season doth he then bring forth,
The fruits of righteousness;
His leaf is full and evergreen,
His toils are richly blest.

Not so are those ungodly men
Who like the chaff are blown;
For by the wind they are removed
To regions dark and lone.

The way of godly, righteous men,
Is known and blest of God;
But He will bring to naught the way
Which wicked sinners trod.

⁓⁓

Motives For Holy Zeal
Our foes have sought to bring us down
With fervor night and day;
But God has been a constant friend,
More vigilant than they.

What motive, this, to serve our God
Devotedly each day!
He overcomes our enemies
And turns their darts away.

Their zeal for their pathetic gods
Burns like a raging fire;
And should we not serve heaven's God
With zeal that burns much higher?

For us our Lord laid down His life—
He cares for us always;
Do we not then owe Him our all,
All our remaining days?

⁓⁓

Redeem the Time
The years roll on incessantly,
And time doth take its toll;
With every breath we older grow,
And swiftly near our goal.

May we redeem the time with care,
And serve our Master well;
That we might be a fruitful bough,
And in His favor dwell.

Treasures Above

The fleeting charms of earth soon fade,
They quickly pass away;
Hence we await with longing heart
The joys of endless day.

This world is no sure dwelling place,
The winds of change are strong;
All nature speaks to us each hour,
"You shall not stay here long."

Then wisdom would that we should place
Our hopes on things above;
Undue regard for earth will prove
An empty, wasted love.

We cannot serve two masters here,
Our love we can't divide;
'Tis God or mammon we must serve
Which one? We must decide.

The strong appeal of wealth and fame
Has many souls enslaved;
We must be very prayerful if
From this we would be saved.

O may each child of grace be blest
To know and understand,
The only wealth with endless worth
Is in the promised land.

Set your affections, saints of God,
On things beyond this earth;
Such treasures will not fade away,
Nor ever lose their worth.

❧

A Bridle on the Tongue

Ill-humored words have oft distressed
My mind and soul since I was young;
And I have learned there's constant need
To put a bridle on my tongue.

Harsh words have often pierced my heart;
O how, at times, those words have stung!
And thus I've seen how much we need
To put a bridle on our tongue.

Unguarded words, sharp and unkind,
Oft-times are quick and loosely flung;
O how much better if there'd been
A bridle put upon the tongue!

How often have we spoken words
Upon which little children hung!
And how we later on have wished
We'd put a bridle on our tongue!

How often had our Lord been pleased
If to His teaching we had clung!
Which tells each one of us that we
Should put a bridle on our tongue.

When tongues made pure are loosed in heav'n
Eternal anthems will be sung,
And there will be no further need
To put a bridle on our tongue.

Love Not the World

Set not thy hopes on earthly things,
On things of time and sense;
They yield a short-lived pleasure and
A meager recompense.

Our best-loved treasures of this earth
Will all be left behind;
Why should we set our hearts upon
A world that's so unkind?

Our treasures should be stored above
Where they will ne'er decay;
Where thieves cannot break thru and steal
And take our goods away.

This world can only disappoint,
It has no endless joys;
Its promises of wealth and fame
Are just an empty noise.

Great hosts have followed Satan's lead
In hopes of worldly gain;
But they have found to their dismay
It only brought them pain.

Ungodly men may prosper here,
But they will find at last
That there are no more joys for them,
Their pleasures all are past.

While saints, tho' poor when living here,
Are heirs of heav'n above,
And greater wealth can no man know
Than God's eternal love.

More and Less

Time hastens on, soon we shall sleep
Beneath the chilly sod;
Hence we should use our moments well
And spend more time with God.

More time in meditation sweet
Upon His word divine;
More time in humble, fervent prayer,
Great comfort there to find.

More time in service to the saints
And working for their good;
More time in striving for the right
And living as we should.

More time in seeking holiness,
Less time on worldly gain;
More thankfulness for what Christ did
That cost Him so much pain.

"Less of ourselves and more of Christ,"
Let this our motto be;
Less of the things that cloud our sight
And make Him hard to see.

More singing of the songs of Zion,
Less foolishness and jest;
More of an humble walk with God,
For this is always best.

O help us, Lord, to spend more time
In these more worthwhile deeds;
And grant us less of what we want
And more of what we need.

The Joy of Obedience

How happy is the saint
Who yields his all to God,
And seeks the strait and narrow way
Our blessed Savior trod!

Our Lord is glorified
When we obey His word,
And heed with contrite heart and mind
The gospel we have heard.

Obedience is the way
We show our faith and love;
For otherwise no one can know
The graces that we have.

The child who disobeys
And wanders from his God,
Will be brought low and made to feel
The painful chastening rod.

When we in love obey,
God answers from above
By blessing us to sweetly feel
The tokens of His love.

May we be always true
To His Divine command,
That we may build upon the Rock
And not upon the sand.

'Tis thus that we enjoy
His smiles from day to day,
And have the grace and strength we need
To hold upon our way.

If It Takes the Rod

Troubles make me flee to Thee, Lord,
Sorrows make me seek Thy face;
If I had no sore afflictions
I would never seek Thy grace.

When I'm groping in the darkness,
Then I'm busy seeking light;
And this keeps me ever hoping
That Thou, Lord, will set me right.

If it takes Thy rod to right me
Then withhold from me Thy peace;
If my troubles keep me humble,
Then I pray they may not cease.

I have learned thru hard experience
That my flesh is weak and frail;
If I lean on my own powers,
I am destined e'er to fail.

I must ever trust in Jesus
To sustain me day by day;
To provide, protect, and guide me
Lest my feet should go astray.

When I'm weak then I am strongest
(Weak in *self* but strong in *Him);*
I have tried all earthly helpers,
But I can't rely on them.

All I ask, Lord, is Thy mercy:
Let my chast'nings gentle be;
Whether happy or dejected
Keep me running e'er to Thee.

PART 7
PRAYER & WORSHIP

The Model Prayer
Our Father Thou, which are in heav'n,
Most hallowed is Thy name;
Thy kingdom come, Thy will be done,
In heav'n and earth the same.

O lead us not, most gracious Lord,
Into temptation's way,
But from all evil, now we plead,
Deliver us each day.

Our sins forgive, as we forgive,
And daily bread supply,
For Thine the pow'r and kingdom is,
Forever, Lord, Most High.

Using Our Parts in Worship
With our eyes, we read the word of God,
With our ears we hear the same;
With our heart, we feel its blessedness,
With our lips we praise His name.

With our hands, we labor in His Cause,
With our feet we tread His ways;
A God-given faith underlies it all,
And He receives all the praise.

A Yearning Within

I am compelled to sing of Thee,
Almighty God of earth and sea;
My heart would burst without a song
To Thee who art so great and strong.

The melody within my heart
Doth to my soul great joy impart;
As in a sweet triumphant praise
I sing to Thee throughout my days.

There is a yearning deep within,
My voice with saints to sweetly blend;
And in Thy praise to thus unite
In rapt'rous strains of pure delight.

O Give Thanks

O give thanks unto the Lord,
Whose mercy doth endure;
To Him who made the heavens and
Whose faithfulness is sure.

O give thanks unto the Lord,
Whose mercy doth endure;
For He is full of goodness and
His thoughts and words are pure.

O give thanks unto the Lord,
Whose mercy doth endure;
Who by His blood redeemed His own
And was for sin their cure.

Singing in the Spirit

Sometimes the saints sing mournful songs
To suit their somber frame;
At other times they sing with joy,
Exulting in God's name.

With sacred songs they oft' exhort
Each other as they go;
In Psalms and Hymns they sing with grace
As in His love they grow.

Sometimes "The Parting Hand" is sung
And each one's longing heart,
Desires that sweet and happy land
Where saints shall no more part.

O Bless the Lord

"O bless the Lord," my soul doth say,
And may I ne'er lose sight
Of mercy shown, of love bestowed
And of His pow'r and might.

O bless the Lord, and may I not
Betray His sacred trust;
May I be faithful to His Cause
'Till I return to dust.

O bless the Lord, my conquering King,
May I with ev'ry breath,
Extol the wonders of His grace
And praise Him ev'n in death.

My Foremost Desire

O Thou Majestic King of earth
And Ruler of the skies,
With reverence may our heart and soul
In praise to Thee arise.

Thou art all-wise and sovereign too,
No man can stay Thy hand;
Thy people are a num'rous seed,
As countless as the sand.

When I behold Thy holiness,
My soul adores the sight;
Thou art my heart's foremost desire,
My soul's most pure delight.

Restraints Soon Removed

Dear Lord, had I ten thousand tongues,
I could not praise Thee as I ought;
Ten thousand years would not suffice
To tell of wonders Thou hast wrought.

The limits of our present pow'rs
Restrain us all from day to day;
We cannot sing as we would sing,
We cannot pray as we would pray.

But these restraints shall soon remove
And we shall happy fly away;
And in a perfect place of rest
We'll praise Thee in a perfect way.

How Great the Blessings

How plenteous are the mercies of
Our never-failing God!
How precious are His precepts and
How kind His chast'ning rod!

How frequent are His favors t'ward
Such worthless worms as we!
How wondrous that we e'er could have
Such blessings large and free!

How sweet the hope that dwells within
The hearts of saints so dear;
That they will rise one glorious day
And e'er with Christ be near!

How Blest Are We!

How blest are we if we can feel
God's grace on us has been conferred;
How blest if we can understand
A portion of His precious word!

How blest are we if we have felt
The touch of His renewing hand;
How blest if we have had a taste
Of heaven's rich and fruitful land!

How blest are we if we have heard
The gospel's pure and joyful sound;
And if within a heart made pure
The love of Christ doth now abound!

Meeting as One
How grand it is to meet
With saints on earth so sweet;

When all unite as one
In God's beloved Son;

To worship and to praise,
And songs of love to raise;

To hear His word so dear,
And feel His presence near;

For such sweet times we yearn,
And long for their return.

God's Fullness Can't be Told
How gracious is our God!
How precious is His name!
Sound forth His praise in joyful lays
And spread abroad His fame.

He rules in earth and sky;
He turns the hearts of men;
His mighty hand can ne'er be stayed
Nor e'er His goodness end.

Forever shall His name
In heaven be extolled!
His fullness cannot be expressed
Nor e'er be fully told.

Exalt the Lord

Exalt the Lord, Oh soul of mine,
And worship at His feet;
Let heav'n and earth and sea combine
To make their praise complete.

Exalt the Lord, ye much loved saints,
With all thy heart and soul;
Throw off all earthly, vain restraints
And His great name extol.

Exalt the Lord, with ev'ry breath
While anthems to Him raise;
And may we in the hour of death
Yield up our life in praise.

May We Delight in Thee

Eternal God, with awe we view
Thy majesty and grace;
And earnestly we long to see
The smilings of Thy face.

When Thou dost speak the angels pause
And listen to Thy voice;
To do Thy will is their delight
And therein they rejoice.

O may we too find sweetest joy
As to Thy words we cling,
And of the wonders of Thy grace
May we forever sing.

Thankfulness

Give thanks to the Lord all ye saints
For blessings too great to describe;
Be constantly giving Him thanks,
And honor to Him thus ascribe.

Be thanking Him when you retire,
And thanking Him when you arise;
True thankfulness ne'er should expire,
For it is pleasing in His eyes.

We owe Him all the thanks and praise,
And more, than we can ever give;
So let us thank Him all our days
And serve Him humbly while we live.

❧

A Debt of Praise

A never ending debt of praise
I owe, O God, to Thee;
A debt from which I do not wish
To ever be set free.

I want to praise Thee ever more
On earth and then above;
I cannot praise Thee, Lord, enough
For Thy eternal love.

How little do I serve Thee, Lord,
While bound in sinful clay!
I long to render *perfect* praise
And see a *better* day.

Put words of praise within my soul,
Lord, I beg of Thee;
Melt my cold heart with heav'nly love
That I may purer be.

O leave me not in darkness, Lord,
To struggle and to grope;
But let me lift my voice in songs
Of love and joy and hope.

My days down here are few, dear Lord,
May they not run to waste;
But let me praise Thee and enjoy
Of heav'n a sweet foretaste.

O what a debt of love I owe,
I never can repay;
I'll be *forever* praising Thee
Throughout an endless day.

O, Let us Praise Thee

O gracious Lord, 'tis our desire
To glorify Thy matchless name;
Who by Thy blood hast purged our sins
And covered all our wretched shame.

O let us praise Thee and extol
The wonders of Thy mighty love;
And may around us often fall
Sweet gospel showers from above.

With humble hearts we bless Thy name
And seek for grace to rightly sing,

To worship in a hallowed frame
And pleasing sacrifice to bring.

O let us feel Thy presence sweet
As once again with saints we meet;
And may we live down at their feet
And often find the mercy seat.

O may our lips and lives express
Our love for peace and righteousness;
And as we travel toward Thy rest,
In all our ways Thy name confess.

And when we near our final place,
May we live out our failing days
With full assurance of Thy grace,
And in our hearts a song of praise.

We Owe Him Our All[1]

To our boundless Lord, all glory belongs;
Let praises ascend, in each of our songs;
His glory exceeds all the pow'rs of our mind
And when we look deeper, more glory we find.

We're lost in the depths, of this endless mine
Of His inspired truth, in each treasured line;
O, thank Thee, Great Father, for Thy precious word
Both written and spoken and blessedly heard!

We ne'er could repay, the debt that we owed,
Nor thank Thee enough, for blessings bestowed;

---

[1] This poem may be sung to the tune of "O Worship the King," No. 8 in the *Old School Hymnal, Eleventh Edition.*

Thy greatness and goodness no tongue can portray,
Nor amply expound on the great coming day.

We owe Thee our all, for all Thou hast done
In giving us life, through Thy darling Son;
Thy mercies are boundless, Thy love without end,
How little of Thee can our minds comprehend!

O, keep us by grace, while we dwell below,
And help us each day, to learn and to grow;
Help us to be strong when affliction abounds
And e'er to be faithful when evil surrounds.

O, help us, dear Lord, to praise and adore,
And thus to extol, Thy name ever more.
And when life is ended may we then arise
To dwell in perfection with Thee in the skies.

Bless His Great Name[2]

Christ is my chief delight; bless His great name;
He gave me life and light; bless His great name;
When I was dead in sin, He placed His grace within
Where only dross had been, bless His great name.

He taught my heart to fear; bless His great name;
Then made His promise dear; bless His great name;
He brought me to His feet, and made His mercy sweet,
Now I with joy repeat, bless His great name.

O, may I ne'er forget; bless His great name;
He paid my awful debt; bless His great name;
Now praise to Him I owe, long as I dwell below,
Then homeward I will go; bless His great name.

---

[2] This poem may be sung to the tune of "Heaven Is My Home," No. 381 in *Old School Hymnal, Eleventh Edition.*

When Gathered to Worship

Dear Father in heaven, before Thee we kneel,
To bring our petitions and make our appeal;
We come empty-handed and longing for bread,
And waiting with patience until we are fed.

Of worth we have nothing before Thee to plead,
But as beggars we come in our weakness and need;
So hungry and faint we approach Thee this day,
And beg that we not be sent empty away.

May Thy name be extolled by Thy servant's sweet voice,
And the whole congregation be blest to rejoice;
Bless the sick and the weak who desire to attend,
And abide near their hearts to uphold and befriend.

Let us go from this place on the strength of Thy word,
And in sweet meditation on things that we heard;
Help us walk close to Thee till again we unite,
Whether here in this place or in heaven's pure light.

To God Be the Praise!

To God alone belongs the praise
For everything of worth;
For any blessings we might name
In heaven or in earth.

Yes, He alone deserves the praise
For life and breath and health,
For any good that we receive,
For any temp'ral wealth.

To Him alone all praise belongs
For all our joyful songs,
And visits from His Spirit sweet
For which our bosom longs.

All praise to God for saving grace,
And for His darling Son
Who died that we might live with Him
When life on earth is done.

Let all our praises be to Him
And none to feeble man;
For none can question what He does
Or stay His mighty hand.

O, ye who love this Blessed One,
Praise Him with heart and mind;
For 'tis alone in Him that we
Our all in all shall find.

❦

The Lord's Passover
Precious are those hallowed moments
When we feel the Lord is near,
As we gather 'round His table
Filled with reverential fear.

We partake of bread unleavened
And of wine in one accord;
This we do in sacred mem'ry
Of our broken, bleeding Lord.

We recall the Lord's Passover
In that dark Egyptian night;
Giving Israel sweet deliverance
From their sore and wretched plight.

Now our Lord is our Passover
(Look with wonder at the cross);
See Him bleeding for His people,
See Him purging all their dross.

Bless us, Lord, to feed upon Thee
As we by Thy grace are led;
May Thy word to us be precious,
More than life or daily bread.

Take us in Thy care and bless us
Ever to extol Thy grace;
Help us live in humble union
And to meekly fill our place.

As to Thy House We Oft' Repair[3]

Lord, may our hearts with pleasure glow
As Thy great mercies to us flow;
O, may we more devotion show
And bless us more of Thee to know.

As to Thy house we oft repair,
O, condescend to meet us there;
Bless us to feel Thy presence dear
And to Thy bosom draw us near.

Give us fresh tokens of Thy love
And set our hearts on things above;

---

[3] May be sung to the tune of "The Doxology," No. 3 in *Old School Hymnal, Eleventh Edition,* or "Old Hundred," No. 488 in *The Good Old Songs.*

Let us once more rejoice in Thee
And more of Jesus let us see.

When we depart Thy house this day,
Lord, keep us safely on our way;
And bless us soon again to meet
With Thee and at each other's feet.

Divergent Seasons

Often preaching seems an empty, lifeless chatter,
With no depth of feeling or of matter;
But when God indicts a sermon in the heart,
It is manna to the soul right from the start.

There are times we go to meeting without praying,
And we find no life in what the preacher's saying;
But at other times we go with hearts a'pleading
And the preacher says just what our souls are needing.

We would all do well to keep our eyes toward heaven,
And remember from whence all good things are given;
What a burden any duty can seem to us
If the Lord is not around us, in, and through us!

May we learn to live more closely to our Savior,
And be always watching closely our behavior;
For if we are not oft' seeking for His blessing
We will find our days are often more distressing.

Though our failures often have our tears o'er-flowing,
Yet we have a precious hope of a home-going;
Where we'll no more be our sorrows here a'voicing,
But will ever be with Christ in heaven rejoicing.

A Prayer for the Preachers

Bless, Lord, those saintly men who stand
And bravely preach Thy word;
Who will not compromise thy truth
Nor yield to threat or sword.

Give courage to these faithful souls
When Satan hurls his darts;
That they may faithful e'er remain
And comfort fainting hearts.

When feeling cold and dead and dull,
Lift them again on high;
That they may feed thy precious flock
And thy name glorify.

Help them through storm and cold and heat
To overcome each blast;
And when they hurt, Oh help them, Lord,
On Thee their cares to cast.

Help them to walk in duties way,
And good examples lead;
Bless them to comfort grieving souls
In all their hours of need.

Let Thy great name be magnified
When they Thy word proclaim;
And everything they say and do,
Extol Thy precious name.

And when they reach their journey's end,
Let them lie down in peace;
And go where joys shall never end
And pleasures never cease.

A Prayer for the Aged

Look down with special care, Dear Lord,
Upon the aged saints;
And give them frequent respite from
Their often sore complaints.

When little things become a mount,
Then hear their feeble plea;
That all those mountains may remove
And be cast in the sea.

May they grow stronger, Lord, in Thee,
The weaker they become;
And sweeter be their thoughts and dreams
Of their eternal home.

When feeling lonely and unloved,
To them, Dear Lord, draw near,
To fill the aching void they feel
And to allay their fear.

Help them to call to mind the past
And mercies they've enjoyed;
And may in thoughts of future bliss
Their minds be oft' employed.

Encourage them when days are glum
And help them look above;
And give to them from time to time
Fresh tokens of Thy love.

And then when life is ebbing low
And coming to an end,
Enfold them in Thy warm embrace
As sweetly they ascend.

At the Lord's Table

'Round Thy blest table, Lord, we meet
And then we wash each other's feet;
May we forever have a seat
Where there is fellowship so sweet.

At this dear table so divine,
We are so favored there to dine;
Thus feasting on the bread and wine—
All praise and honor, Lord, is Thine.

Thy body and Thy blood so dear
Compel our hearts to thus draw near;
But we approach with godly fear
And shed the penitential tear.

In sweet remembrance, Lord, of Thee,
Who died upon the cursed tree,
We come, we hope, on bended knee
Thus more of Thee to hear and see.

Until Thou dost once more appear,
We hope to humbly gather here
At Thy great table without fear
Sweet gospel truths again to hear.

And then at last we hope to dine
Upon eternal bread and wine;
And none shall ever there repine
But ever bask in joy sublime.

The Church

The church a comfort doth provide
The saints while here below;
It's like a shade in summertime,
A shield from every foe.

A place for saints to join in praise
Away from scorner's glare;
A place where gospel truth is preached
And each for others care.

A place where love flows breast to breast
And thrills each humble heart,
And in a precious hope in Christ
Each member feels a part.

Communion time, that solemn feast,
With reverence they partake,
In honor to Christ's sacrifice
Made for His people's sake.

They long to meet, to greet, to pray,
And sing the songs of praise,
And hear of God's eternal love,
The Great Ancient of Days.

A place of labor, yet of rest;
A place to serve as one;
To dwell in bonds of fam'ly love
Until their journey's done.

Thank God for such a lovely place,
So solemn, yet so sweet;
A foretaste of that church above
Where all the saints will meet.

Fear Not, Little Flock[4]

The souls of those who seek for wealth,
The Lord shall soon require,
But riches which are stored above
Shall never there expire.

Fear not, little flock—fear not;
Thy Father knows thy need;
Fear not, little flock—fear not;
He will His children feed.

Behold and see how lilies grow;
They do not toil nor weave;
Yet kings in all their royal dress
Are not arrayed like these.

Fear not, little flock—fear not;
Thy robe is sparkling white;
Fear not, little flock—fear not;
The Savior is your light.

If God so clothe the forest green,
Whose leaf will soon be gone,
Shall He not much more glorify
His chosen and foreknown?

Fear not, little flock—fear not;
Thy God is on His throne;
Fear not, little flock—fear not;
He'll come and take you home.

[4] Copyright □ 1983 by Old School Hymnal Co., Inc. and published as No. 481 in *Old School Hymnal, Eleventh Edition.* Used by permission.

Think on Things Above

O saints of God, look up, look up,
And think on things above;
And contemplate with grateful hearts
The wonders of God's love.

Reflect upon thy low estate—
Thy guiltiness and sin;
Where wouldst thou be if not for grace?
How sad thy state had been!

Consider all the Lord has done
For thee through all thy years—
How many times He drew thee nigh
And wiped away thy tears!

How many times He bore thee up
When thou wast bending low—
How often He protected thee,
There is no way to know!

How many turns thy thoughts might take
Reflecting on His grace;
As providential mercies flood
Thy mind with rapid pace.

A thousand reasons He has giv'n
To praise His name for aye;
And not the least is His great love
That never fades away.

A Prayer in Rhyme

Almighty God of truth and love,
Look down from Thy great throne above
And grant my humble plea.

Unworthy though I am, Dear Lord,
Help me to walk in sweet accord
With those who follow Thee.

Let me not wander from the fold,
But humbly walk with those of old
Who ever faithful stood.

And when the storm clouds hover o'er,
Help me to trust Thee all the more
And seek Thee as I should.

When earthly cares come like a flood,
Help me to think upon Thy blood
And all the pain you bore.

Let me find comfort in the thought
Of what Thy blood for me has bought,
And love Thee even more.

And when my fading sun has set,
I'll ne'er again complain or fret
But praise Thy name for aye.

In that sweet home prepared of old
For all Thy chosen, favored fold,
In perfect endless day.

PART 8
THE WORD OF HIS GRACE

God's Precious Word
Majestic Lord, so grand, so pure!
With Thee our heart resides;
Our all in Thee doth rest secure,
Our soul in Thee confides.

Upon Thy word we can depend,
And all the saints have found
That when Thy truth we comprehend,
We never are let down.

Each word of Thine is pure, dear Lord,
Its truth we've come to love;
Its writers were with one accord
Inspired from heav'n above.

Thy word, O Lord, is fully tried
And has come forth as gold;
If ev'ry part were amplified,
What volumes would be told!

Thy word is settled, firm and sure,
Forever, Lord, in heav'n;
And in this truth we rest secure—
It was Divinely giv'n.

It is a lamp unto our feet,
A light unto our way;
Its meditations, O how sweet!
Its comforts ne'er decay.

Our hearts are awed by this great word,
And in it we rejoice;
And whether it is read or heard,
It speaks with mighty voice.

The Greatest News
Scarce could there be a greater joy
Than that which heralded our King;
While shepherds kept their flock by night,
They heard the heav'ns with praises ring

"All praise to Him Who dwells on high,
And on earth peace, good will toward men."
And this the saints still deem today
The greatest news there e'er has been.

Rejoicing in God's Word
We cannot comprehend God's pow'r,
Nor fathom His decree,
Nor know how He can make a world
By saying, "Let it be."

But divers truths have been revealed
In His inerrant Book;
And we are blessed to oft' rejoice
As on its page we look.

310

A Treasure

Thy word, Dear Lord, a treasure is,
With priceless truth replete;
Its cheering themes delight the heart,
Its promises are sweet.

It drips with heaven's crystal dew;
Its fragrance is Divine;
It speaks of Thy majestic deeds
Wrought by a pure design.

O may we take this precious truth
And hide it in our heart—
Esteem its value more than life,
And never from it part!

The Sea Of Truth

Our finite minds—so dimly lit—
Of things divine can little know;
The wisest men, with knowledge great,
Still have vast room to learn and grow.

The sea of truth spreads great and wide
Before our oft' inquiring eyes,
And who can tell the precious depths
Which 'neath its sparkling surface lies?

Teach us, Dear Lord, out of that store,
The lessons we most need to know;
That we may live and serve aright,
More love to Thee and others show.

The Sacred Word

How pure the sacred word of God!
How full of truth divine!
How precious to the hungry soul!
How rich each treasured line!

It is a light unto the path,
A lamp unto the feet,
Of ev'ry soul who loves the Lord
And longs with Him to meet.

O let us search this word each day
For guidance and for light;
That we may better serve the Lord
And worship Him aright.

God's Inspired Word

Dear Lord, without Thy precious word,
What pleasures we would miss!
How often would we grope for light
And say, "What meaneth this?"

How puzzled would we often be
Without Thy inspired Book!
We would not know Thy saving work
By mercy undertook.

How blest the hands that wrote the words
That guide us ev'n today!
We thank Thee, Lord, for giving us
This lamp to light our way.

Given From Heaven
The precious word of God
By inspiration given,
Doth edify and comfort us
With sacred things of heaven.

Instruction such as this
Could only come from heaven;
And truth so lovely, so sublime,
In mercy must be given.

O may we keep this word
Exactly as was given;
And let it be our daily guide
Till we are safe in heaven.

Cease Not My Soul
O soul of mine, cease not thy trembling
Before God's pure, inerrant word;
And oft with saints be thou assembling
Where songs and prayers are sweetly heard.

Cease not, my soul, from seeking mercies
Freely bestowed from God's great hand;
While my glad heart and mind rehearses
His prior blessings great and grand.

Cease not, my soul, from calm reflection
Upon the precious things above;
And oft be found in self-inspection
Casting thyself upon God's love.

God's Unsearchable Truth

God's truth a mighty ocean is
With borders vast and wide;
So great no man can search the depths,
Nor see from side to side.

God's truth is high, so very high,
No man can span its height;
It is a fountain infinite,
An endless source of light

O blessed truth! How precious 'tis!
It feeds the hungry soul;
On earth we only know in part,
The half has ne'er been told.

The Gospel

When the gospel's joyous message
Is proclaimed with power divine,
Hungry souls are fed and watered
As upon its truth they dine.

When expressed with true conviction,
And with power from on high,
This sweet gospel gives them comfort
As their souls to Christ draw nigh.

Wondrous message of redemption!
May we hear it oft' proclaimed!
Let it be alleged and opened
And to sinners thus explained.

Divine Riches

We may never have great treasures
Such as kings and princes hoard;
But we have unbounded riches
In the bank of heaven stored.

As joint-heirs with Christ our Savior,
We have wealth beyond compare;
And it cannot be corrupted,
For 'tis safe in heaven's care.

All the wealth of earth together
Can't compare with truth divine;
Nor with just one glimpse of Jesus,
And a sip of heaven's wine.

The Star of Truth

O guiding star point us to Christ
And may we wise men be;
May we draw nigh to Him by faith—
O what a Friend is He!

His word is our bright star of truth,
It points us e'er to Him;
And like the magi may we search
And find great joy like them.

To Jesus' feet is where we come
When following the light—
The star of truth that shows the way,
And leads our steps aright.

The Truth

A knowledge of the truth,
O what a precious gift!
O blessed, blessed truth,
It gives the heart a life!

The truth will set you free
From many hurtful things;
God's children all agree,
Great comfort oft' it brings.

Thank God for truth so dear;
By Him it was inspired!
Of hearing it with cheer,
Poor sinners ne'er grow tired.

❦

A Vast Gulf of Truth

Countless volumes have been written
Of the mighty works of God;
Yet so much lies deeply hidden
In this gulf so vast and broad.

Mortals grope for revelation,
Yet how little do they learn;
With no mind for Inspiration,
Things divine they can't discern.

Only as God lifts the curtain
Can they know such truths of grace;
None can know such things for certain
Save for those with godly taste.

❦

Pearls of Truth

If God to thee has been revealed
So as to make thee mourn,
Then pearls of precious truth are thine
And should thy walk adorn.

Cast not these pearls before the throngs
Of unbelieving men;
For they will rend you with their words,
And will not turn from sin.

These pearls belong to humble souls
To whom God's grace is shown;
Who know and feel their wretchedness
And trust in God alone.

A Word to the Preacher

O, Elder friend, when thou dost rise
To speak in Jesus' name,
May His good Spirit rest on thee
To make thy tongue a flame!

Lay out for us in words of love
The wonders of His grace;
That we by faith may eat His flesh
And view His lovely face.

O tell us more about our Lord
Who is our Chief Delight;
Expound to us His precious word
And tell us of His might.

Proclaim His mercy, large and free,
And make His praise thy theme;
And show to all that His great work
Is not a failing scheme.

O tell us more of His great truth
And guide us in His way;
Let all thy words point us to Him
Who is our Hope and Stay.

O may thy words drop like the dew
And flow into our soul;
And may God's truth ring true and clear
And fly from pole to pole.

Show us our sins, though it may chafe,
For we wish not to stray;
And in those things wherein we fail,
We would not therein stay.

Preach on, dear brother, thru the storms,
Till death shall still thy tongue;
Portraying visions of that land
Where saints are ever young.

The Book of Books

To search the word of God each day
And humbly meditate and pray,
Will yield much fruit in knowledge gained
As well as wisdom thus obtained.

This Book of Books is truth divine,
And we should search each treasured line;
To every query it gives light
And cheers the heart of those with sight.

When seeking troubled hearts to calm,
We often op'n it to a Psalm;
And by still waters we find rest
As in green pastures we are blest.

How oft' have saints perused this Book
And riches from its pages took;
And oft' found use for what it said
As by its teachings they were led!

Oh! Book divine, thy sacred page
Doth oft our hungry souls engage;
Thank God! Thank God! for truth so sweet,
So full, so rich, and so complete!

May we more often search its lines,
To stir and lift our better minds;
And ev'n when dying may its truth
Assure us of eternal youth.

Yes! Let us oft to God's Book turn,
That we may better grow and learn;
It will inspire more upward looks,
This treasured gift! This Book of Books!

O, What a Foundation!
Through all the ages of the past
God's word has proven sure;
And though the pow'rs of hell assail,
It ever shall endure.

No jot or tittle of His truth
Shall ever be destroyed;
For that which Wisdom hath decreed
Can never be made void.

Upon His word we can rely—
Much comfort may be found
In knowing that it cannot fail
Nor ever let us down.

PART 9
THE PASSAGE OF TIME

A Lesson of Time
The present year has taken flight
And we should view it as a sign,
That we not love this present world,
For soon we'll leave it all behind.

Reviewing the Past
Another year is closing fast,
And we review the recent past;
God's word again has proven true:
Our days are evil, swift and few.
But day by day His grace was shown,
And by His grace He'll lead us on.

Thanksgiving and Supplication
For mercies shown throughout the year,
We thank Thee, Lord, most high;
And in the days that lay ahead,
Would'st Thou to us draw nigh.

May we Thy righteous name adore,
Who giveth life and breath;
And thus our all to Thee consign,
And praise Thee ev'n in death.

A New Start
Another year before us lies,
A time to start anew;
With fields so white to harvest, and
With laborers so few.

May each of us take up our cross,
And bear our rightful part;
Enduring all for Jesus' sake,
With soul, and mind, and heart.

Another Year

Another year has come and gone,
And we begin anew;
Would'st Thou, O Lord, give strength afresh,
And see us safely through.

And as we face the days ahead
May we not fear to stand;
To faithfully proclaim Thy truth,
And honor Thy command.

Fret Not Time's Passage

Why should it make us gloomy
That years pass swiftly by,
When each day draws us nearer
To pleasures in the sky?

Why should the day's swift passage
Be cause to us for grief,
When at its peaceful ending
Awaits a sweet relief?

There is a day a'hast'ning
When toils will all be o'er;
O may time swiftly wing us
Where time will be no more.

The Time is Short
"Our days are like a passing shade"
That "withers like the grass,"
A "Vapor" that soon fades away—
Our nights, like lightening, pass.

The years go "swifter than a post,"
"They flee away" in haste;
We have but just a moment here;
We have no time to waste.

"Redeem the time," the Word declares,
Be faithful "while it's day;"
"The time is short," "the fields are white,"
We soon shall pass away.

~~~

Use Time Wisely
How swiftly do the sands of time
Pour through the hour-glass;
We count grandfather's chimes and say
"Much time is lost—alas!"

Why do we squander precious time?
Past moments come no more;
O help us, Lord, to use time well,
Until our time is o'er.

~~~

Time

Time—thou art ever on the wing,
Swift as a stone shot from a sling;
Thou hast an unrelenting gait—
For no one wilt thou hesitate.

Time—swiftly hast thou tolled the years,
Marked by our joys—stained by our tears;
Thou art a healer in God's hand,
Thou canst run well, but canst not stand.

Thou canst be wasted and abused,
Thrown to the winds or wisely used;
Thou art a gift we mortals need,
Whilst thou art ours let us take heed.

Christ shall return, we shall ascend,
He knows the hour thou hast an end;
When earth is burned thy day is o'er,
In Heaven's world time is no more.

PART 10
MISCELLANEOUS POEMS

Bless Thy People, Lord
O great God of our salvation,
Bless Thou our beloved nation;
Protect it from its enemies,
Both on the land and on the seas.

The hatred of a wicked world
Is now, in mass, upon us hurled;
But Thou canst stay their evil hand
And help Thy people bravely stand.

Be with Thy faithful servants, Lord,
That they may live in sweet accord;
For otherwise they cannot stand,
Nor dwell within a peaceful land.

A Nation Gone Astray
This once-great country, free and brave,
Has surely lost its way;
It's now alright to break God's laws,
But very wrong to pray.

To pass out contraceptives in
The schools is quite okay;
To teach (safe sex?) is quite alright,
But never dare to pray!

The devil preaches loud and long,
"From church you ought to stay;
The Lord is really not concerned —
It does no good to pray."

"Perverted lifestyles now are fine,"
Our President doth say;
And then he goes on Sunday morn,
And proudly claims to pray.

"What is the answer?" many ask;
And this the Scriptures say,
"God's people ought to look to Him —
Return, repent and pray."

This country rose to pow'r and might
With God's almighty aid,
Because good men, with noble hearts,
Bowed openly and prayed.

Dear God, in mercy now come down,
And move the clouds away;
Restore our souls, preserve our land,
And help us all to pray.

About My Wife

In Nineteen Hundred Sixty-one
The Lord gave me a precious wife,
To be a vital part of me—
To be a special friend for life.

She bore my little boy and girl
And nurtured them as mothers do;
She gave them all she had to give
While being faithful t'ward me too.

Down thru the years she's stood by me—
She's been the perfect preacher's wife;
She's given me her heart and soul—
So much delight, so little strife!

She's mingled with both rich and poor
And been a friend alike to all;
She's held her preacher's feeble hand
As he has answered heaven's call.

She sewed his buttons, ironed his shirts,
And such like things too large to tell;
That he might go among the saints
And represent his calling well.

And all of this without complaint,
With loving heart and willing mind;
Not many like her has God made,
"A virtuous woman who can find?"

I thank Thee, Lord, for giving me
This faithful, precious, loving bride,
To share my joys, my tears and griefs,
And always with me to abide.

Bless her, O God, with special grace—
She has a special, loving heart;
And may we walk together, Lord,
Until at last in death we part.

AUTHOR'S BIOGRAPHY

R alph Edward Harris was born on August 24, 1938, the middle son of the late Elder Horace Edward Harris and Lela Wells Harris.

He united with Bethel Primitive Baptist Church near Bonifay, Florida on April 19, 1959, at the age of twenty. His father baptized him on May 3, 1959, in Holmes Creek at Vernon, Florida.

On December 13, 1959, he was called on to speak for the first time in the name of the Lord. Bethel Church liberated Brother Harris on October 1, 1960, and a presbytery ordained him on April 1, 1961, at the age of twenty-two years.

Elder Harris was joined in marriage to Melba Diane Jones of Edison, Georgia on December 24, 1961 at Mars Hill Primitive Baptist Church near Edison. His father officiated the wedding.

Ralph baptized his new bride into the fellowship of Bethel Church on April 1, 1962, and later had the pleasure of baptizing both his children, a sister-in-law, an Uncle, a daughter-in-law, and numerous others.

Elder Harris has served several Primitive Baptist churches in some capacity over the course of the past fifty-four years of gospel ministry. These include *New Mt. Zion*, near Samson, Alabama, *Enterprise Church*, Enterprise, Alabama, *Antioch*, Texasville, Alabama, *El Bethel*, Tampa, Florida, *Harmony*, Barwick, Georgia, *Corinth*, Red Level, Alabama, *Pleasant Hill*, Graceville, Florida, and *New Home*, Red Level, Alabama. He was also blessed to see his son, Bridgman, also called into the ministry and to see him successfully serve as pastor of three churches.

Brother Ralph began suffering with asthma in infancy and has lived with this disease and related ailments since then. His constant struggles with illness, and the burdens and conflicts, some of which were associated with the work of the ministry, taught him at an early age what it was to "endure hardness," far beyond what most of those who knew him have ever realized. But in spite of his trials, he is always mindful of the fact that God's mercies to him far exceeded anything he could ever have asked or thought, and the words of Jacob in Genesis 32:10 are a precise expression of his inner most feelings: "*I am not worthy of the least of all the mercies, and of all the truth, which thou hast showed unto thy servant.*"

He considers his dear wife who always stood by his side through all the checkered scenes of life to be one of the greatest blessings God has ever bestowed upon him, apart from Divine life and light. He has always felt, and often says, that one of the greatest miracles on earth is a good Primitive Baptist preacher's wife, and that God has given him one of the best. "She is," said he, "an answer to my prayers, for I began early in life begging the Lord to give me a companion who would be suitable to my needs in whatever station in life I might be required to fill."

Elder Harris has never sought a place for himself in the ministry, fully believing that the only place he could be successful in his efforts, or be of any real service or value to God's people was in the place in which God put him. During his more active years, he traveled in over twenty States preaching in a great many churches and declaring the glorious doctrines of the gospel as preached by Christ and His apostles and faithfully adhered to through the centuries by the Primitive, or Original, Old School Baptists.

In late 1975, Elder Harris was asked by the Board of Trustees of the *Advocate and Messenger* to assume editorship of that publication, which was a Virginia-based Primitive Baptist periodical dating back to January, 1854. He prayerfully agreed to comply with their request and the Lord blessed him to serve in that position until failing health made it necessary for him to retire from that labor of love in December, 2009, a thirty-three year span of faithful service.

A 385 page book of Elder Harris' religious articles entitled *Day by Day* was published by *Sovereign Grace Publications* in 2012. These articles were selected from writings that he composed during the fifty-plus years of his ministry and published in various Primitive Baptist papers.

It is our pleasure, now, to add to that prose work this volume of poetry. Though the two titles do not exhaust the full extent of his edifying mind and prolific pen, we trust that together they will prove a worthy legacy to the labors of a godly minister whose life has been so wonderfully employed by God to the blessing of His church and people.

www.ingramcontent.com/pod-product-compliance
Lightning Source LLC
Chambersburg PA
CBHW060327100426
42812CB00003B/899